INDIAN CURRENCY

AND

RESERVE BANK PROBLEMS

INDIAN CURRENCY
AND
RESERVE BANK PROBLEMS

BENOY KUMAR SARKAR

GYAN

Published by

Gyan Publishing House
5, Ansari Road
Daryaganj, New Delhi-110002
Phone: 011-47034999, 9811692060
E-mail: books@gyanbooks.com

Distribution Network
gyanbooks.com
India, USA, Canada, UK, Australia, France

ISBN: 978-81-212-8620-6 (PB)
First Published, 1933

2nd Impression 2023

Printed at: Gyan Press, Delhi.

INDIAN CURRENCY AND RESERVE BANK PROBLEMS
Author: Benoy Kumar Sarkar

INDIAN CURRENCY

AND

RESERVE BANK PROBLEMS

INDIAN CURRENCY
AND
RESERVE BANK PROBLEMS

BY

BENOY KUMAR SARKAR

Post-Graduate Departments in Economics and Commerce, Calcutta University; Hony. Professor of Economics and sometime Rector, College of Engineering and Technology, Jadabpur, Calcutta; *Gast-Professor an der Technischen Hochschule*, Munich (1930-31): *Membre correspondant de la Société d'Economie politique* (Paris); *Corrispondente al Comitato Italiano per lo Studio dei Problemi della Popolazione* (Rome); Editor, *Arthik Unnati* (Economic Progress).

SECOND, ENLARGED EDITION

N. M. RAY-CHOWDHURY & CO.,
11, College Square, Calcutta.

1934

Price Re. 1-8

CONTENTS

CHARTS

The Hilton Young Currency Commission's Report

(August 1926)*

The reform of Indian currency was the subject of acute controversy towards the end of 1925 when Professor Sarkar returned to India after an absence of nearly twelve years in foreign countries, in some of which (France and Germany) he had the chance to study post-war currency and banking developments on the spot in connection with his University and other academic appointments. He was therefore called upon to take part in formal and informal discussions at Bombay, Benares, Allahabad, Lucknow and Calcutta. As soon as the Report of the Hilton Young Currency Commission was published in the summer of 1926 he was interviewed by *Forward* (Calcutta) and his observations were published on August 4.

GOLD STANDARD

Questioned as to whether he is in agreement with the recommendations of the Currency Commission's Report, Prof. Sarkar remarked:

"In the main, the Report seems to inaugurate an epochmaking landmark in our monetary history. My remarks, based as they are on a bird's-eye view of some of the summaries published in different dailies of day before yesterday, can however be nothing but impressionistic. I should like to single out one or two prominent features of the proposed scheme, namely, the following:

"1. The policy of the gold standard will certainly bring India up to date and in line with the latest currency reforms in Europe.

"2. The gold currency although not yet in contemplation is not definitely outvoted.

"3. The idea of issuing "saving certificates" redeemable in 3 or 5 years in legal tender money or gold will be appreciated by a large section of the country as a mode of investment and thus be ultimately conducive to economic development.

"4. The most revolutionary item in the proposal appears to be the one relating to the cessation of coinage of silver rupees. This implies

*From Sarkar: *Greetings to Young India* (Calcutta, 1927).

that (a) more small denomination notes will be issued and (b) the ground will be prepared for the gold currency at some future date. And this will involve automatically the training of the people on a large scale in habits of using money without any metallic basis and ultimately also in the use of banking and other credit instruments.

RESERVE BANK

Questioned as to whether he agrees with any of the points raised by Sir Purushottamdas Thakurdas, Prof. Sarkar said:

"I do not agree with Sir Purushottamdas who believes that the present Imperial Bank of India should have been made into the proposed Central Bank. It is desirable that the new institution should not function to any large extent as a commercial bank but like the Bank of England or the *Reichsbank* of Germany look chiefly to the currency problems of the country. This new institution, namely, the proposed Reserve Bank of India, is likely to be a powerful instrument in the establishment of India's credit and financial system on advanced lines, such as have been experimentally found to be sound in the currency policy of the Great Powers. I think that this is one of the most important items of reform in the present Report.

"It may be remarked, in passing, that the Committee wish this new institution to be more or less a duplicate of the British institution by recommending that the Issue Department should be kept wholly distinct from the Banking Department.

RATE OF THE RUPEE

1. The stabilization of the Rupee at 1s. 6d. (and not at 1s. 4d.) such as is being recommended by the Committee has, indeed, for some time been a phenomenon of the balance of trade. To a certain extent, this higher exchange certainly is an incentive to the purchase of foreign goods by the Indians, since the prices in terms of £ sterling will appear rather cheap to persons possessing the Rupee. This, however, is not an unmixed evil because, situated as we are, we cannot afford to do without foreign goods. In reality, we do not possess many manufactures. It is desirable, therefore, in the interests of millions of consumers, especially of such as cannot get their immediate necessities supplied by the industries near at hand, to obtain the goods from abroad at comparatively lower prices. Besides, the industrialization of Indian agriculture as well as other economic functions will need machineries and chemicals, such as can be furnished mainly from abroad. To get these things compara-

tively cheap is really a great help to the *Swadeshi* (Home Industry) Movement.

"2. But, one may ask, is not this cheapening of foreign goods on the Indian market detrimental to our growing *Swadeshi* industries or, for that matter, to all those industries that are being run on Indian soil with Indian or foreign capital? To a certain extent, yes. But we must note that today in India there is a Tariff Board and that the Government is committed to the policy of promoting the "key industries" within Indian boundaries. Whenever, therefore, our countrymen feel that certain industries are not in a position to maintain themselves on account of foreign competition, there is a likelihood of getting some protection for them in one form or other, by means of agitation and legislation.

"3. The tariff policy will thus to a certain extent counteract the evils such as they are of the currency policy."

Higher Exchange and Indian Agriculture

(January, 1927)*

Early in January 1927 were held in Calcutta a session of the Indian Industrial and Commercial Congress, in which business men from different parts of India took part, as well as a session of the Indian Economic Conference, the association of the University economists of India. At both, Prof. Sarkar was invited to participate, and some of his interpretations on the issues involved were presented in a lecture before the second association (3 January). He said in part as follows ;

EXCHANGE AND EXPORTS

"There are certain considerations bearing on the rate of exchange which seem to have been ignored or overlooked as much by the Majority Report of the Hilton Young Currency Commission as by Sir Purushottomdas Thakurdas in his Minute of Dissent as well as by those who have contributed to the controversy during the last five months. The brunt of the fight has been borne by the problem as to the extent of adjustment or mal-adjustment between the Indian price-level and the world price-level.

"But I intend to invite the attention of economists and publicists to the subject of the Rupee-Sterling ratio in relation to the balance of trade. My object is to discuss the problem of Indian exchange in the context of export-curve and import-curve, and more especially, the question of exports as affected by higher exchange.

The eighteen-penny Rupee is being condemned on the ground that it is detrimental to India's export-industries, in other words, to the interests of agriculture and the cultivators. My way of looking at things is quite otherwise.

PRICE IN RUPEES

Theoretically speaking, it may indeed be conceded to deductive reasoning that as soon as the Rupee becomes high compared to Sterling,

*From Sarkar : *Greetings to Young India* (Calcutta, 1927).

the foreigner has to pay more in Sterling for the Indian goods if the price be calculated in Rupees. In other words, Indian goods become dearer to the parties that have to make purchases with Sterling. The consequence should be a fall in the foreign demand, which is tantamount to saying that the exports will tend to diminish in quantity. This tendency to the diminution of exports on account of high exchange (or deflation) has indeed constituted the argument of all those economists and statesmen who in almost every post-war country, in Austria, in Czechosolvakia, in Germany, in France, in the Balkan states, in Italy, and even in England have advocated inflation (i.e. lower exchange) in order to furnish a stimulus to exports.

PRICES IN GOLD

"Now, you would retort that this holds good in the relations between "gold standard" countries. But in "gold-exchange standard" countries like India you might argue that the prices of export-goods are calculated not in the currency of the country itself, i.e. not in Rupees but in terms of the international medium of exchange, viz. gold, say, dollar or sterling. And therefore as soon as there is high exchange the Indian exporters, in other words, our agriculturists should have to be satisfied with a lesser number of Rupees for the same amount of goods because Sterling is low compared to the Rupee.

Thus arguing, we should expect agriculture to be a less and less profitable concern and the agricultural output diminishing in quantity. The natural consequence to international trade should not fail to make its appearance. It ought to manifest itself in the tendency of India's exports to diminish.

DEFLATION IN THEORY AND EXPORT-STATISTICS

We thus come to the same position as we had in the previous consideration. That is, whether the prices of Indian exports be calculated in terms of gold or in terms of Rupee, a high exchange—the eighteenpenny Rupee,—should prove to be a damper on India's export-trade.

These, then, are two wings of the *a priori* theory, the speculative reasoning, old Ricardian logic, on the strength of which one might argue that deflation (or high exchange) as embodied in the eighteen-penny Rupee would adversely affect India's export-trade, and therefore, the agricultural classes. But what are the actual facts of India's overseas trade? We have the figures to tell us that exports have neither declined in volume during the last decade or so nor have they yielded a lesser and lesser number of Rupees.* In other words, agriculture has not

**Review of the Trade of India in* 1924-25 (Calcutta), Tables Nos. 7, 28—41.

proved to be an economically losing concern nor has the agriculturist suffered.

INCREASE OF EXPORTS IN GRAIN AND SEEDS

The war-average in the export of grain (rice, wheat, barley etc.) gave the figure 3,141,000 tons. In 1923-24 it rose to 3,429,000 tons and in 1924-25 to 4,260,000 tons. And the total Rupee prices received by Indians rose from 344,180,000 to 508,715,000 and 650,604,000 respectively.

The essential seeds were exported to the extent of 708,000 tons per year during the war-period, 1,177,000 tons in 1922-23, 1,255,000 tons in 1923-24 and 1,328,000 tons in 1924-25. And the Rupee yields for the corresponding years were 121,742,000, 273,538,000, 298,172,000 and 331,685,000 respectively.

The total value of exports, again, does not indicate any tendency of decline. On the contrary, beginning with Rs. 2,159,670,000 per year during the war-period, it successively rose to Rs. 2,991,619,000, 3,488,301,000 and 3,846,653,000 in subsequent years.

THE EXCHANGE-CURVE (1922-25)

But we are not interested in the export-curve in its splendid isolation. We are out to understand the export-schedule in reference to the rate of exchange. What is the significance of these rises in exports in the currency-history of India? Let us, therefore, place these increases in the figures (both in volume and Rupees) for exports in the perspective of the exchange-curve during the corresponding periods. All this time, as we are aware, the Rupee has been steadily rising in relation to Sterling. From 14, 3/6d. in July 1922 it rose to 14, 27/32d. in December 1922, 15, 1/8d. in July 1924, and 18, 1/6d. in June 1925.

The situation, therefore, is curious. The exports have been increasing both in volume and Rupee-price at a time while exchange has been rising too. But our theory should lead us to expect quite the reverse, namely, a decline in exports with the rise in exchange.

EXPORT INDIFFERENT TO EXCHANGE

The facts being what they are, the conclusion forces itself upon us in a rather unexpected form. There is no other way but to believe that the amount and Rupee-value of India's exports are not necessarily dependent upon the rate of exchange, to put it in a sober manner. And therefore it would not be right to tie the fortunes of the cultivator and the exporter inevitably down to the currency questions. Agricultural prosperity, in so far at least as this export-item is concerned, has shown itself supremely indifferent to the 12½% or 15½% fluctuations in the Sterling-Rupee relations.

If there is any thing definite to be deduced from the history of our foreign trade it is the anomaly, the paradox, that the higher Rupee has actually been a stimulus to export or rather that the period of high exchange has coincided with the period of increased exports. What, then, becomes of the theory? We have to admit that the demand for India's goods abroad is not determined, if at all, exclusively by the rate of exchange. There are other and more weighty circumstances influencing the price-movements of export-goods.* And it is necessary to conclude that the validity of the purchasing power parity doctrine in Indian conditions has been as limited or modified as that of the quantitative theory of money.

*Cf. p. 12.

The Reserve Bank Bill, 1927

On August 19-21, 1927 the District Young Men's Conference was held at Dacca with Professor Sarkar as President of the Economic Section. His presidential address, delivered in Bengali, was entitled "The *Artha-Shastra* or Economics of Young Bengal" and dealt, among other topics, with the Reserve Bank Bill as published in the Gazette of India Extraordinary, January 17, 1927. The paper was summarized in English for the *Journal of the Bengal National Chamber of Commerce* (of which he is the editor) for September, in which, besides, some of his other views on the question have appeared from time to time without necessarily binding the Chamber to them.

The following paragraphs are extracted from the *J.B.N.C.* :

SHAREHOLDERS' BANK ACCEPTABLE

"On the question as to whether the proposed Reserve Bank is to be a state institution or a shareholders' institution we should remember that while the former type is represented in Bolshevik Russia, Italy, and elsewhere the latter is to be found in Great Britain, France, Germany, U.S.A., Japan and other countries. In regard to the administration of the Bank, Indianization should certainly have to be pressed with as much emphasis as possible. But one need at the same time observe that Indianization is unknown in any sphere of governmental activity in British India.

INDIAN BANKS IGNORED AND AGRICULTURE NEGLECTED

"There are one or two technical items in regard to the constitution of the Bank on which it is desirable to suggest an amendment in the final drafting of the Bill. First, a good many of the joint stock banks, "Loan Offices" and *Nidhis* under purely Indian management should be granted the privilege of having their commercial papers recognized by the Reserve Bank. The Bill in its present form does them great injustice for while it recognizes all the twenty one foreign banks it has accorded the same privilege to only five Indian concerns. Secondly, the co-operative credit societies of India, especially the central co-operative banks should also be admitted to the same privilege. Besides, one of the conditions to be imposed on the Reserve Bank should be similar to that by which the *Banque de France* is compelled to advance large credit to the co-operative agricultural institutions on exceptionally favourable terms.

NOTE-ISSUE ON GERMAN LINES

"The conditions according to which the note-issue of the Reserve Bank is to be regulated are in the main acceptable. The Bill has followed neither the rigid system of the Bank of England nor the ultra-liberal system or absence of system of the *Banque de France* in regard to the gold-cover for notes. The fundamental principles of the *Reichsbank* of Germany, elastic as they are, on which have been later founded to a certain extent the Bank of Italy and the Federal Reserve Bank of America are to be noticed in the Bill relating to the proposed institution for India.*

THE POSITION OF BENGALIS

"The Bill that has been introduced in the Legislative Assembly at Delhi in order to constitute a Reserve Bank of India enumerates in a special schedule 26 banks at present operating in the country. The promissory notes of these institutions, supported by documents, have been considered by the Legislative Department to be good security against which the proposed Reserve Bank may be authorized to make loans for fixed periods not exceeding 90 days. Of these 26 institutions only five are Indian, viz. the Bank of Baroda, the Bank of India (Bombay), the Central Bank of India, the Indian Bank (Madras) and the Punjab National Bank. It is evident that there are no Bengali institutions competent enough in the present judgment of the authorities to deserve a place in the schedule."

*See "The Remaking of the Reichsbank and the Banque de France" in Sarkar: *Applied Economics* Vol. I (Calcutta 1932) and "Currency Reform, Gold Standard and Reserve Bank" (*Banca d'Italia*) in his *Ekaler Dhana-Daulat O Artha-Shastra* (The Wealth and Economics of Our Own Times) Vol. I (Calcutta, 1930).

Re the French cover according to the new principle see Art 4 of the Act of 25 June 1928 in Lebeau: *La Banque de France* (Paris, 1931), pp. 327-328.

The Linking of the Rupee with Sterling

(November 1931)

The linking of the Rupee with Sterling constituted the burning topic of the day when towards the end of October 1931 Professor Sarkar returned to India after two years and a half of sojourn in Great Britain and the Continent, during which period he was Guest-Professor for two semesters at the *Technische Hochschule* (Technological University) of Munich as well as a President of the Economic Section of the International Congress on Population held at Rome. On his arrival in Calcutta, he was interviewed by the *Amrita Bazar Patrika* and his observations on the Rupee-Sterling question were published in the issue of Nov. 4.*

BRITAIN'S GAIN

Commenting on the linking of the Rupee with Sterling Prof. Sarkar said:

"Great Britain will gain relatively on the Inidan market in comparison with America, Germany, Japan and other gold-standard countries. It is likely that the British percentage of India's foreign trade will rise a few points above the last few years' average of 30 to 40 per cent.

"It is to be observed that while Great Britain gains, India does not lose. It is an instance of Great Britain gaining at the cost of other foreigners.

"Exports from India are likely to rise. The agricultural classes of Bengal and other provinces may be expected to derive considerable benefit.

FALL OF THE RUPEE

"The explanation is as follows. Great Britain's getting off the gold standard is tantamount to the depreciation (inflation) of the British currency, namely, Sterling, in terms of the gold-standard currency. The linking of the Indian currency with the British implies (1) that the ratio of the Rupee to Sterling remains unchanged, i.e. what it has been since

*Somewhat expanded for the present publication.

1927 but (2) that the Re. is depreciated to the same extent as the £ in terms of the dollar, the Reichsmark, the yen, the franc and other gold-standard currency units.

"To give a concrete instance. Suppose previous to the linking the Re. was equal to RM. 1·50. Now let us say for the simplicity of calculation that the Re. is equal to RM. 1·00 only. In other words, the fall of the Rupee in terms of the German currency, or the rise of the RM. in terms of the Re, has been assumed to be as great as 33 1/3 per cent. Previous to this change (i.e. depreciation on the one side and appreciation on the other) the Germans could buy one Rupee worth of our jute with RM. 1·50. But after the change they are in a position to buy the same one Rupee worth of jute with only RM. 1·00. There is thus a great inducement offered to the Germans to buy our jute simply because of the alteration in the currency relation. On the other hand, previous to the change Indian customers could buy RM. 1·50 worth of German machineries with only one Rupee, whereas after the change with the same one Rupee they can import only RM. 1·00 worth of machineries from Germany. In other words, Indians find German machineries too expensive, and Germany is compelled to lose much of the market for her goods in India.

FALL IN IMPORTS FROM GERMANY, JAPAN AND AMERICA

"On account of the depreciation or fall of the Rupee American, German, Japanese and other gold standard people will find Indian goods cheaper to buy with their currency than before, whereas Indians will find the goods of American, German, Japanese and other gold standard countries dearer to buy with Indian Rupee or British Pound than before. Exports to these countries will therefore tend to rise while imports from them will tend to decline.

"But in so far as the relations of trade between Great Britain and India are concerned, the linking will leave the British buyers or sellers *vis-à-vis* Indian sellers or buyers in the relatively same position as before. Indian goods will not appear cheaper to the British customers nor will the British goods appear dearer to the Indian customers,—because neither does the Rupee fall in relation to Sterling nor does the latter rise in relation to the former.

NO LOSS TO INDIA

"Great Britain's goods will enjoy a relative advantage in India for no other reason except that the American, German, Japanese and other gold-standard goods will appear comparatively dearer to Indian customers. Great Britain's gain in this instance does not spell India's loss. In so far as India is bound to import a certain amount of foreign goods,—machineries, apparatuses, chemicals etc.—for her daily requirements and in order to promote the development of her manufactures the competition between Great Britain and her non-British rivals on rather advantageous terms to herself is, other circumstances remaining the same, of no special economic significance to India.

"These are the purely theoretical considerations* based on the significance of the present currency readjustments. But in the mean time, one does not know as yet as to how in order to counteract or neutralize the discrimination in favour of Great Britain's goods America, Germany, Japan and other gold-standard countries are likely to manipulate their currencies or take other measures. Besides, as long as the *Swadeshi* movement is on in India and opposition to British goods continues to inspire the patriotic sentiments of the people it is certainly difficult to foresee to what extent the discrimination involved in the currency legislation is likely to act effectively in favour of Great Britain."

**Cf.* p. 7. The fall of the £ and Re has been followed by the fall of the Yen since 14 December 1931 and the fall of the Dollar since 20 April 1933.

Currency and Imperial Preference vis-a-vis Indian Peasants

(April-May 1933)

At the commencement of the eighth year of *Arthik Unnati* (Economic Progress), the economic monthly in Bengali, Prof. Sarkar as editor presented a survey of the previous seven years (1926-33) in the issue of April-May 1933. Among other topics the bearings of currency and tariff with special reference to Imperial Preference on the agricultural classes of India were discussed by him in a concise manner. The following paragraphs are reproduced in English from this survey:

INCREASE IN EXPORTS

"The eighteen-penny Rupee was introduced in 1927. As a result of this measure the Indian cultivators' goods have not been sold abroad in relatively less quantities than before, as feared at the time. A comparison of the export figures of 1927-31 with those of 1923-26 will indicate rather that the exports have increased in jute, cotton as well as tea, and this in spite of the fact that on account of the world depression we should rather expect a relative or even absolute diminution. Besides, the export of those oil-seeds the demand for which in foreign countries is old and regular has also shown some increase. The standpoint of those Indian publicists and economists who carried on the agitation against 1s. 6d. and in favour of 1s. 4d. has been demonstrated to be too pessimistic.

LINKING BENEFICIAL

"In September 1931 the British pound fell. The Indian currency was at once attached to the British as a tail. Consequently the Rupee fell along with Sterling. Since then in terms of the German, American, French, Italian, Japanese and other gold-standard currencies there has been a depreciation of the Indian monetary unit. It is because of this fall of the £ st. and of the Rupee that the industrial goods produced by the British manufacturers and the agricultural produce of the Indian cultivators have been exported to foreign countries in relatively larger

Review of the Trade of India in 1931-32, Tables 7, 28-41.

amounts, of course, *within the limitations of the world-depression.* Our peasants would have been in a bad fix without this affiliation or linking. In the interests of our cultivators it should be expedient for us to have the Indian currency linked up with the British in future also. The Rupee should rise and fall along with Sterling in terms of other currencies.

GOLD EXPORT DESIRABLE

"Since 1929 on account of the world-depression the goods of all agricultural countries have been exported in relatively smaller quantities. Agricultural depression is the most outstanding fact of the present crisis.* It is on account of this that great suffering has been caused to the agriculturists of India as to those of other countries. But there are many foreign goods,—machineries, factory-installations, technical equipments, scientific apparatuses, drugs, chemicals, etc., which are absolutely necessary for the Indian people, and these have to be imported by all means although in somewhat reduced proportions.

"It is clear, however, that it has not been possible in recent years, on account of the fall in the demand, to export as much agricultural produce as is necessary to pay for the imported goods. This is why the export of gold bullion has been found to be the most convenient as payment of price for the imports. Had it been impossible for India to ship gold abroad there would have been great hardships among the Indian people.

IMPERIAL PREFERENCE A HELP TO AGRICULTURE

"Towards the end of 1932 reciprocal Imperial Preference was agreed upon at Ottawa with India also as with the other members of the British Empire. In accordance with the terms of this Ottawa Agreement the Government of the United Kingdom levies customs duties on Indian goods at lower rates than on foreign (i.e. non-British, non-Indian, non-Imperial) goods. One may naturally expect under these circumstances an expansion of market in the U.K. for Indian goods. Had there been no preference coming to us from the British side Indian cultivators would have had to suffer *relatively great* losses. As soon as the world-depression is effectively over,† new marks of prosperity for the Indian

*On the world's agricultural depression see André Pavie : "La crise agricole et mondiale" in *Bulletin de la Société d' Economie Politique de Paris* for January 1933 and G. Masci : "Considerazioni sull' indebitamento agricolo" in *Rassegna Economica* (Naples, May 1933).

†For the analysis of circumstances such as are likely to lead to business recovery in India by autumn 1934 see Sarkar ; "Economic Planning for Bengal" (*Insurance*

peasants will tend to make their appearance. By 1940, i.e. the terminus of the Preference period, we may expect some positive and solid signs of material advance among our agricultural classes."*

and Finance Review, Calcutta, March 1933). For some of the symptoms see in this connection the curves for the United Kingdom in the *Monthly Review* of the Midland Bank (London, August-September 1933). cf. also the improving situation of Germany as registered in the *Wirtschaftliche Mitteilungen* of the Deutsche Bank und Disconto Gesellschaft for September 1933.

*A detailed analysis is to be found in the author's forthcoming book entitled *Imperial Preference vis à vis World-Economy* (In relation to the International Trade and National Economy of India).

Tariff and Currency Problems at the World Economic Conference, London

(May, 1933)

In regard to the World-Economic Conference held at London in the summer of 1933 Prof. Sarkar, as editor of the Bengali monthly *Arthik Unnati* (Economic Progress), made the following among other observations:

"We witness here the clubbing of the intellects from some sixty different countries. A congress of this dimension was never held in the world before. But those economic theorists or economic statesmen who are expecting extraordinary results out of these deliberations are bound to be disappointed. On the other hand, those economists and publicists who are used to and capable of making an objective survey of the conditions up to which the world has advanced in the different corners are not likely to feel pessimistic or heart-broken about the eventual services of this Conference.

SEVERAL TARIFF-UNIONS

"In the first place, as regards tariff arrangements in international trade it should be understood that a free trade regime is out of the question. The system of customs duties and these, again, of a more or less highly protective character, is bound to continue. But it is not unlikely that in certain geographical areas a number of regions or races may consider it advisable to establish *Zollvereins* or customs-unions. The British Empire has shown the way, the French Empire is likewise showing the same way.*

NO WORLD-CURRENCY

"In the second place, there is the question of the world's currencies. Certain theorists and even statesmen have been making propaganda in

*See the series of articles entitled "Est-il opportun de réunir une Conférence Economique Coloniale?" in *Journal du Commerce* (Paris) for 30 March 1933.

favour of what may be called an international currency such as is likely to be legal tender throughout the world. One should not attach much importance to such ideas or projects. It is undoubtedly true that the regime of technocracy has succeeded in promoting business movements and intercourse between the most diverse and distant nooks and corners of the world. But the establishment of this world-economy has not been able to induce the growth of the international or universal state as commanding sovereignty over all the races and regions of the world. Mankind continues still to be polycentric in political organization. The currencies of the world also will continue to be diverse. A world-currency is not yet a question of practical politics.

DIVERSE CURRENCY-UNIONS

"Currency is like tariff mainly a political category. The state is therefore the chief consideration in currency questions. In the world-economy of to-day the following six statal organisms deserve special mention :

1. The British Empire,
2. The French Empire,
3. The U. S. A.
4. Soviet Russia,
5. Japan, and last but not least,
6. Germany.

"But it is not on the strength of politics (i.e., race and nationalism) alone that mankind can go on. The other states of the world are bound to get connected with these centres by economic ties in spite of their own nationalistic ambitions as well as of the nationalistic achievements of the big centres. No matter whether these other regions are from the standpoint of political sovereignty independent, semi-independent, or dependent there is no means of their flourishing in the economic fields without linking with some one or other of these powerful centres. It is only when the tariff and currency systems of these other peoples are managed in intimate unison with those of the six systems enumerated above that the avenues to their economic progress will be clear and smooth. In other words, currency-unions will have to become the established fact of the world-economy just as the customs-unions are. But in any case, the nationalistic rivalries and antagonisms of the political organisms are so complicated and so frequent that one ought to remain prepared for occasional, nay, periodical disruptions and reshufflings of customs-unions and currency-unions.

GOLD BULLION STANDARD

"There is hardly any likelihood of gold losing its prestige in the world's currency questions. For some long time yet the international monetary world will continue to witness the prevalence of the Gold Bullion Standard which has been introduced in the leading countries (including even India) since 1924-26. We do not for the time being find any ground for altering the regime of that standard. It is to be observed that in reality currency difficulties have not arisen in many countries during the period of the world-economic crisis since 1929. The chief cause or mark of the present depression is to be found in the decline in the exports and imports of goods. The crisis is not mainly one of currency but of commerce, especially, of international trade."*

MULTIPLICITY OF STANDARDS

"It is not to be taken for granted, indeed, it is hardly likely that the terms of affiliation, linking and assimilation between the region and the powerful centre will be along the same lines in the diverse currency-unions of the world. In each of these currency-unions the relations of the central currency with the affiliated currencies are bound to remain diverse. In certain regions we may have to encounter perhaps the monometallic silver standard and in other instances it is not surprising that the "dyarchy" of gold and silver i.e. bimetallism will prevail.

NO CHANGE IN RUPEE-STERLING RATIO

"The terms of affiliation or understanding between India and Great Britain in regard to currency matters are in the main beneficial to our people and should be adhered to for some time. In case the further depreciation of the Rupee is considered desirable in order to raise prices at home or promote the export of goods a corresponding depreciation of Sterling will be a necessity in order that the currency-union may be kept in tact. The tariff relations of India in regard to the United Kingdom being what they are (Imperial Preference), a change in the Rupee-Sterling ratio will be prejudicial to India's interests unless of course at the same time the tariff schedules are revised from top to bottom.

SILVER-CURRENCY AND LOWER GOLD-COVER AS HELP TO RISE IN PRICES

"In order to solve the world's price-problem, i.e., to raise the prices to a higher level, it may be found expedient to enable the Reserve

*Roberts: "Gold Movements into and out of the United States" in *Selected Documents on the Distribution of Gold* submitted to the Gold Delegation of the Financial Committee (League of Nations, Geneva 1931), p. 56.

Banks of every country to issue a comparatively larger volume of notes. This will necessitate the modification of the laws relating to these Banks. The modification is to be effected in the direction of authorizing the issue of notes against a lower than the statutory percentage of gold-cover. It may be possible in the same connection to elevate poor silver back to the legitimate currency level. As a result, silver may again rise in international worth. The enhancement of the agricultural prices by such currency measures, desirable as it is for our peasants, landowners, middle class men and the Government, will at the same time enable India to buy larger quantities of foreign machineries; and this will serve to bring down the unemployment figures of the machinery-producing countries also."

The Export of Gold from India

(May 1933)

On May 28, 1933 a paper on India's contribution to international trade was read at the *Bangiya Dhana-Vijnan Parishat* (Bengali Institute of Economics) by one of the Research Fellows, Sj. Sudha Kanta De, M.A., B.L., translator of Ricardo into Bengali. It was followed by discussions in which several other Research Fellows as well as Dr. Narendra Nath Law, who had been a Government of India delegate to the Round Table Conference in London, took part. One of the points debated had bearings on the export of gold from India.

To this discussion Prof. Sarkar, as Director of researches at the Institute, contributed the following observations:

"Much sentimentalism has of late been showered on this outflow of gold. But to the student of matter of fact economics it is hardly worth while to be so emotional about gold as such. And in regard to the actual place of gold in Indian economy the positive facts are such as should counsel us to be less nervous and fidgety than we happen to be at the present moment.

GOLD BULLION AS WEALTH

"Gold bullion is only a form of wealth. As such it is not necessarily more important or valuable than other forms of wealth. Agricultural holdings or farms, pastures, mango groves, paddy fields, grass lands, tanks, fisheries, mines, crops, cattle, coal, iron, machineries, chemicals, buildings, silver, bank notes, cheques, shares, securities, etc. are, as forms of wealth, not of less worth than gold. To possess large quantities of one or other of these forms of wealth is to be rich in the same sense as to possess large quantities of the yellow metal.

GOLD BULLION ORDINARILY NOT MONEY

"For the purposes of commercial intercourse there is no reason why each one of these diverse forms of wealth could not be used against one another as equivalents. A system of barter-economy would indeed lead to the establishment of every form of wealth as money or instrument of payment.

"It is just an accident that certain precious metals, especially gold and silver, happen to be used as the standard of value in most of the countries of the world at the present moment. It is an accident also that along with coins struck off from precious metals the cheques, notes, securities etc. have by fortuitous circumstances of the modern world-economy obtained the privilege of functioning as instruments of payment in commercial intercourse. All the other thousand and one forms of wealth including the gold and silver bullions (as contrasted with coins) function to-day as mere goods, and however valuable they may be, are not allowed to function as money.

GOLD BULLION AS EXCEPTIONAL INSTRUMENT OF PAYMENT

"If then, India has to make any payments abroad she must use either the coins as struck off according to law (not the bullion pieces) or the cheques, notes, etc. Unluckily since Great Britain's, and along with her, India's getting off the gold standard, all these usual media of payment have fallen in value in comparison with the gold standard currencies. This depreciation of the currency in its ordinary forms is indeed the result and meaning of the suspension of the gold standard. In order to pay for imports India has, therefore, to discover a way which will not compel her to incur loss by using depreciated currency.

"The best way is naturally to make payment by exporting goods. But on account of the world-depression since 1929 the demand for Indian goods has fallen off in just those countries to which India has to make payments. It is to be observed *en passant* that for the daily requirements of her life as well as in the interest of industrialization India has still to import certain goods (no doubt in reduced quantities) from these countries, although these latter are not in a position to import as much agricultural produce and other raw materials as before. The way of payment by export of goods is then blocked. The only way that is left under the exceptional circumstances is the export of gold bullion, the commodity which has maintained its value in fact by the world standard, or rather has experienced a relative "appreciation". Gold bullion has thus been elevated to the rank of an exceptional instrument of payment, so to say. Such is the case likewise with certain agricultural countries in recent years, for example, Argentina and Australia, in which imports have risen and exports fallen.

THE GOLD IMPORTS OF SEVEN YEARS (1923-30)

"Fortunately for us, India happened to possess gold in quite considerable amounts. From 1923 to 1930 India imported large quantities of gold.* The value of the net imports of gold bullion (deducting the exports) is given below :

	Rs.
1923-24	292,100,000
1924-25	738,800,000
1925-26	348,600,000
1926-27	194,000,000
1927-28	181,000,000
1928-29	212,000,000
1929-30	142,200,000
Total ...	2,108,700,000

During the seven pre-depression years India was in a position to absorb from abroad Rs. 210 crores and 87 lacs.

"And it is this gold which was imported from abroad on account of certain trade relations that is in part being exported abroad to-day on account of certain other trade relations. In other words, as soon as the export and import of goods between India and the foreign countries are restored to the pre-depression level the journey of the same yellow metal back to India may be expected as a matter of course, unless of course in the meantime India chooses to possess some other forms of wealth in order to replace gold imports.

The recent exports of gold* can be shown as follows :

1932	$195,765,000
1933 (May)	$ 51,315,000
Total ...	$247,080,000

During this entire period except only during the last few weeks the Rupee was depreciated and fell from the parity of 46·50 cents to a general level of some 27 cents. At this rate of exchange 247 million dollars would be roughly equivalent to Rs. 940,000,000. This, then, measures the total export of gold as against the import of previous seven years valued, as it is, at Rs. 2,108,700,000.

GOLD BULLION AS NOTE-COVER

"One might suspect that the export of gold would lead to the depletion of gold and thus threaten the gold-cover of the notes issued by the

*For gold imports into India see *Balances of International Payments* (League of Nations Memorandum, Geneva 1931), pp. 123—124.

*For gold exports from India see *Federal Reserve Bulletin* (Washington D. C.) for June 1933, p. 375.

Currency Department. But the story of the note-circulation indicates that the position of the gold reserve has hardly been affected except in the favourable direction. On May 15, 1932, for instance, against a note-circulation of Rs. 1,678,631,000 the percentage of metallic (i.e. gold as well as silver) reserve was 71·79. But the gold bullion accounted for only 6·2 per cent of the total note-circulation. On May 15, 1933 the total metallic reserve was 77·30 per cent of the notes which amounted to Rs. 1,754,990,000.* The percentage of metallic cover has risen from 71·79 to 77·30 per cent. At this latter date the gold bullion as cover for the notes was Rs. 262,604,000 (as against Rs. 106,143,000 on May 15, 1932). And this is 14·9 per cent of the total circulation. The percentage of gold cover has thus risen from 6·2 to 14·9 per cent during the period of the export of gold from India. One need not therefore be too panicky about the situation."

*Indian paper currency returns may be seen conveniently in the weekly *Commercial Gazette* (Calcutta).

Indian Reserve Bank Committee's Report

(August 1933)

The Report of the Committee on Indian Reserve Bank Legislation was published in a summary form on August 4, 1933. On the subject of the proposals contained in this Report Prof. Sarkar was interviewed by *Advance* and his observations and interpretations were published in the issue of the next day, as follows :—

"The principles of the Reserve Bank for India, as first proposed in 1927, appeared to me acceptable from the standpoint of purely banking considerations. There is nothing in the proposals of to-day which can dissuade one from accepting it, provided one does not make too much of formal political considerations.

Unfortunately the items published to-day are so scrappy that it is difficult, except in a very general manner, to call attention to some of the prominent features.

THE AMERICAN SYSTEM

"To begin with, we should be quite clear in regard to the fact that although the new institution is to be called a Reserve Bank there is not much in common between the one proposed for India and its namesake in America, except only in so far as the principle underlying the cover for note circulation is concerned.

"The American Federal Bank is a genuine Bank of Banks, because none but Banks can become members of the federal system; whereas the Reserve Bank for India shares are not to be the exclusive monopoly of banking institutions. Private shareholders should appear to be preponderant, and since no individual shareholder can exercise more than ten votes, the emancipation of the institution from the authority of "big capital" is likely to be realised, at any rate, in theory.

"Although economic India is a territory of vast dimensions, the proposed Reserve Bank will, however, be more akin to the British, French and German institutions, since, by statute, there is no compulsion to derive their shares exclusively from banks as foundation members. The promoters and "proprietors" of the Indian as well as European Reserve

Banks are thus not necessarily banks but business people and other holders of capital.*

RELATION WITH BANKS

"In regard to the relations between existing banks and the proposed Reserve Bank, it seems that, other circumstances remaining the same, arrangements with the Imperial Bank could not *in general* be different from what has been suggested. As for the other banks the principle that they should maintain minimum balances with the Reserve Bank is quite in order. It has been observed by custom in England for a long time, in fact, this is the British "tradition". The *Reichsbank* also has grown into a central station for the deposits of the German banking institutions, although not to the same extent as the *Banque de France;* and of course, in America there is a statute which compels all member banks to contribute a certain percentage of their own capital to the capital stock of the Reserve System.

"All the same, not even in the United States, and not of course in Germany, has it been possible to centralize the deposits and control the risks in an effective manner, because a very large number of banks in those countries lies outside the Reserve System. Besides, many of these banks take part in industrial under-writing, which is very difficult to control as a matter of course.

"DISCOUNTING" PRIVILEGE

"This problem is likely to acquire a special significance in India because the "scheduled banks" such as may have the privilege of having their papers discounted by the Reserve Bank are very few in number. There are no details forthcoming yet, but it is necessary to suggest that in each of the five areas businessmen should see to it that a good many of the Joint Stock Banks, Loan Offices or *Nidhis* under purely Indian management, acquire this privilege.

"We may recall that in the Bill of 1927† *not more than five "Indian" Banks* were to be accorded this privilege as against all the 21 foreign banks of those days. This is a point which is to be approached by us not only from the stand-point of Indianization and political importance

*See Sarkar: "Types and Tendencies in American Banking" in the *Journal of the Bengal National Chamber of Commerce* for June 1927.

†The privilege of "scheduled banks" is not defined in the Report under consideration. For the purpose of the present interview we may commence with the definition as in the Bill of 1927 (discounting privilege). But in the Bill of 1933 the definition of the privilege is substantially different (signature privilege). Cf. pp. 8, 9, 30.

in commerce, but also in order that the business interests of our diverse districts and rural areas can be safeguarded.

MOFUSSIL BANKS

"It is reported that the criterion on which an institution is to have a place among scheduled banks has not been decided upon. I should suggest that it is desirable to attach more importance to deposits than to the paid-up capital in this regard. In this connection, something ought to be done also to link up the "indigenous bankers" of the Mofussil with the entire Reserve system by establishing some legal contact between them and the leading institutions in each area.

COVER

"Something like the principle of 20 p.c. gold-cover has been proposed. This should seem rather revolutionary, because the latest principle in the system of proportional cover,* as embodied in the leading Central Banks of the Continent and America, has been that of between 30 and 40 p.c. But this may eventually be in keeping with the current tendencies with regard to the gold-silver problem that has influenced world-economy during the present crisis. The reduction of gold cover, and the utilization of silver, both for purposes of cover as well as for currency, should appear to be some of the measures calculated to raise the prices and facilitate the rehabilitation of exports and imports on the pre-depression level.

"For the purpose of clarity it is to be observed that the total cover recommended in the Report is 20 per cent gold *plus* sterling-exchange, silver and securities. It is worth while also to note that since August 1930 the actual gold cover of the note-circulation in India has ranged as a rule between 18 and 16 per cent, i.e., somewhat lower than the proposed 20 per cent. The total *metallic* cover, however, has during the same period ranged between 80 and 75 per cent.

INDIA AND EMPIRE-ECONOMY

"It seems to me that our businessmen need not contest this Bill, although it is being thrust upon us rather too hastily. It is clear, at any rate, that the question of ratio remains closed so far as India and Great

*For legal reserve requirements of foreign central banks see *Federal Reserve Bulletin* (Washington, D.C.) for July 1932, pp. 437—438.

Britain are concerned. The currency as well as tariff questions do not, therefore, have to be touched at the present moment. Besides, on account of the Ottawa Imperial Preference India is a part of the Empire-Economy. The Indian economic conditions are not likely to be adversely affected so far as the extra-Empire business relations are concerned, simply because the Bank is established. Of course, when the Federal Structure begins to function, it may be necessary to introduce certain changes in the administrative machinery of the Bank or even reopen the ratio and tariff questions without in any way affecting the principles of central banking as such.

AGRICULTURAL INTERESTS

"From the standpoint of agriculture, it is necessary to observe that the Government ought to get certain concessions from the Reserve Bank in the manner of the French Government from the *Banque de France*,* so that it may be possible to help forward the Co-operative Societies with substantial grants and loans at favourable rates.

"Thus considered, the question of the Directorate deserves more than a passing notice. It is not enough to say that eight directors will represent the shareholders. We should rather stress the point that a substantial portion of the Directorate should represent the agricultural interests",

*For loans without interest to the Government see *Compte Rendu* of the *Banque de France* for 1933 (Paris), pp. 21—22. *Cf.* p. 33.

The Reserve Bank of India Bill, 1933

In view of the discussions on the Reserve Bank Bill by the Joint Select Committee commencing at New Delhi on 23 October Prof. Sarkar was interviewed by the news agency, the *United Press*, on the same day and his interpretations and criticisms from the standpoint of the existing Loan Offices and other joint stock banks under Indian management were published in the leading dailies of India, as follows :—

A BIG AND PRIVILEGED COMMERCIAL BANK

"In the Reserve Bank of India Bill there are certain features which are likely to be interesting to those of our countrymen who wish to see the progress of joint stock banks "under Indian auspices". The Reserve Bank is essentially a commercial bank, and since it is a big institution and an institution enjoying certain privileges from the Government, the ordinary, i.e. private commercial banks have reasons for anxiety in its presence. Even large-sized commercial banks are likely to be upset by the establishment of such a powerful concern. Now, "Indian" banks with solitary exceptions are as a rule medium-sized, nay, tiny or pigmy. As for the eight to nine hundred Loan Offices or "cottage banks," as I have called them so often,* there is every reason for their being nervous about their very existence as soon as the Big One makes its appearance in the market.

"INDIAN" BANKS NOT LIKELY TO SUFFER

"It is just from the standpoint of these fears and anxieties of private banks that we should call attention to the very nature and function of the Reserve Bank as proposed in the present Bill. As in other countries, in India also the Reserve Bank is to be saddled with a statute such as will prevent it automatically from injuring the interests of the private banks. Indian, nay, Bengali banking concerns, as banks, are not likely

*See 'The Bank Capitalism of Young Bengal" in Sarkar: *Applied Economics* Vol. I (1932).

to suffer simply because of the establishment of the Reserve Bank. The safe-guards that have been proposed are extensive and varied and will tend to offer the private concerns, including the Loan Offices of Bengal, opportunities for self-assertion in their own fields. It is to these measures of safety that as students of bank-technique and bank-capitalism our countrymen ought to devote a part of their attention.

RESERVE BANK NOT TO PAY INTEREST

"From the standpoint of private banks the most important clause in the Bill is certainly that which saves them from competition with this privileged institution. The safety of these banks,—large, medium and small, non-Indian as well as "Indian,"—is guaranteed by Art. 17, Section (1), which describes one of the different kinds of business which the Reserve Bank will be authorized to carry on. This has reference to what is called "passive banking," as follows :—"the accepting of money on deposit without interest from and the collection of money for, the Secretary of State in Council, the Governor General in Council, Local Governments, States in India, banks and any other persons."

"The position is emphasized in Art. 19, Section (6), which, while enumerating the different kinds of business forbidden to the Reserve Bank, mentions categorically that it is not permitted to "allow interest on deposits or current accounts."

"On this point the Bill can cite a recent American precedent. The Federal Reserve Act of 1913 has been amended on a large scale by the Banking Act of June 1933* which provides, among other things, for the "safer and more effective use of the assets of banks," and "prevents the undue diversion of funds into speculative operations." Section 19 of the American Act under the present regulations has the following: "No member-bank shall directly or indirectly by any device whatsoever pay any interest on any deposit which is payable on demand."

"Naturally, the Reserve Bank is not likely to attract interest-seekers. The business world therefore is left wide enough for all the private banks and they are thereby enabled to draw upon the resources of everybody who possesses something without fear of competition from this source.

RESERVE BANK BOUND BY ONE, TWO OR MORE SIGNATURES

"Another source of security for the private banks in regard to the question of competition with the Reserve Bank is furnished by Art. 17,

*For the Banking Act of 1933 see *Federal Reserve Bulletin* for June 1933, p. 394.

Section (2). The purport of all these measures is to prevent the Bank from entering into those kinds of "active" business which are likely to be risky in any way. No bill of exchange or promissory note is to be purchased, sold or rediscounted by the Bank unless the documents bear the "signature of a scheduled bank"* as in the case of business in Government securities [Clause (c)] or "two or more good signatures, one of which shall be that of a scheduled bank" as in the case of *bona fide* commercial transactions [Clause (a)] or of agricultural operations or marketing of crops [Clause (b)].

"In all these instences the risks fall ultimately on those institutions which furnish the signature, and it is interesting to observe incidentally that in every instance the "scheduled bank" is either the only such institution or at any rate one of such institutions. Whatever is necessary to safe-guard a Central Bank from the temptations of running headlong into business, which, although likely to be profitable is none the less attended with risk, nay, which is likely to be very profitable *because* it is attended with speculation and risk has been attempted in this Article. The compulsion to consider certain kinds of business only when the guarantee has been furnished by one, two or more good signatures is the greatest brake upon the freedom of the Bank. It is necessarily, therefore, the most desirable in the interest of the private banks because the Bank's competition is thereby reduced to a minimum. The entire world of speculative, risky and therefore profitable business is left free and unobstructed for them and they are at liberty to ransack this world, each according to its risk-bearing capacity.

RESERVE BANK NOT TO MAKE UNSECURED LOANS AND ADVANCES

"In regard to other kinds of "active" business also, the interests of private banks are safeguarded by the Section (4) of Art. 17, which describes the conditions under which the Bank is authorized to make loans and advances. It is provided that the loans and advances must be either repayable on demand or during the period of not more than ninety days. And in no instance are the loans and advances to be made without security. The kinds of security are enumerated in clause (a) to (e), which, however, need not be discussed here. These limitations upon the freedom or discretion of the Bank are further emphasized in Art. 19, Sections (4) and (5), where it is forbidden to make unsecured loans or advances and draw or accept bills payable otherwise than on demand.

*See pp. 8, 9, 25,

"It is to be understood that private banks are subject to no such limitations. They can use their discretion in regard to every proposition that comes, and it is at their free will that they can decide as to whether a client deserves an unsecured accommodation or a credit for longer than ninety days. Indeed, it is just in this power of exercising discretion that the *forte* of banking consists.

THE CLAIMS OF "INDIAN" BANKS

"As regards the status and number of "scheduled banks," the Bill of 1933 is superior not only to that of 1927 but also to that of 1928, because the number of scheduled banks which rose from 26 to 62 in 1928 has risen to 69 in the present instance. In other words, the privilege of "signature," on the strength of which the Bank is to purchase, sell or rediscount bills of exchange etc, has been extended to a large number of "Indian", including some Bengali, concerns. It is to be observed, besides, that the "signature" privilege is substantially different from the "discounting" privilege of 1927.

"The following Bengali banks have been accorded a place in the list of scheduled banks:

1. Bhowanipur Banking Corporation, Calcutta.
2. Jalpaiguri Banking and Trading Corporation, Jalpaiguri.
3. Raikut Industrial Bank, Jalpaiguri.

"The list is not imposing. But one will have to observe that in 1927 not one was mentioned and in 1928 the third in the list of 1933 did not obtain the privilege. But still at the present moment we must not refrain from exploring the possibility of pushing the claims of some more of our "cottage banks" to legislative recognition.

MORE BENGALI BANKS DESERVE RECOGNITION

"It is surprising, indeed, that only three should have been singled out in the Bill. So far as capital-power is concerned, the following institutions belong more or less to the same group as these three :—

1. Jagadamba Loan Co., Birbhum.
2. Indian Industrial Bank, Calcutta.
3. Mahaluxmi Bank, Chittagong.
4. Bengal Central Bank, Calcutta.
5. Luxmi Industrial Bank, Calcutta.
6. Naogaon Atrai Bank, Rajsahi.
7. Chittagong Bank, Chittagong.
8. Jessore Loan Co., Jessore.
9. Tippera Loan Office, Tippera.

The capital of these institutions ranges between Rs. 100,000 and Rs. 500,000.

"And if the criterion is to be furnished by the command over deposits the claims of the following might well be considered along with those of the three in the Schedule;

1. Jessore Loan Co., Jessore.
2. Faridpur Loan Office, Faridpur.
3. Rangpur Loan Office, Rangpur.
4. Bogra Loan Office, Bogra.
5. Bengal Central Bank, Calcutta.
6. Khulna Loan Company, Khulna.
7. Comilla Union Bank, Tippera.
8. North Bengal Bank, Rangpur.
9. Faridpur Bank, Faridpur.

The deposits in these institutions range between Rs. 1,000,000 and Rs. 5,500,000.

"The institutions common to the above two counts are only two in number. Excluding the double entries, then, there are at least sixteen Banks or Loan Offices in Bengal, the claims of which ought to be seriously discussed while preparing the final Schedule for the time being.

While appraising the strength of these institutions, the condition of "frozen assets" in which the Loan Offices find themselves to-day owing to the agricultural depression as an element in the crisis in world-economy should not be treated more seriously in Bengal than in other agricultural countries including the U.S.A.

THE PROBLEM BEFORE BENGALI BANKERS

"It is important to signalize the fact that the present Bill does not, like the one of 1927, make the list statutory and fixed. According to Art. 42, Section (7), the door is open to the Loan Offices of Bengal and the *Nidhis* of Madras as well as other Indian banking institutions to enter the list. The possibility of raising the status of the smaller banks is not to be ignored or minimized.

"Bengali economic statesmen should know how to manage their banking affairs in such a way as to command important position in the atmosphere of the Reserve Bank along with the representatives of other regions in India. Once more let me repeat my suggestion of long standing to the effect that the time has come for amalgamation and consolidation in Bengali banking enterprise. The opportunities to be rendered available by the establishment of the Reserve Bank should be utilized by Bengali bankers in right earnest in order to strengthen their position in Bengal as well as in All-India.

TWO BENGALI INTERESTS NEED SPECIAL DIRECTORS

"The two fundamental interests of the Bengali people in the domain of Indian finance are (1) those of the agriculturists and (2) those of the small-sized banks and loan offices. For some long time to come we Bengalis are bound to remain a nation of virtual peasant proprietors, petty capitalists, small concerns, and cottage or medium industries of diverse kinds such as testify to the new manufacturing talent of Young Bengal in various lines. Our approach to the Reserve Bank must therefore be oriented to these inevitable considerations. From this standpoint we have to see to it that at least two of the eight Directors (in case they are to be eight only) of the Central Board representing the shareholders are persons such as possess special interest in agriculture and small banks. The problem of the directorate, central as well as local, will have to be re-examined from the viewpoint of these basic exigencies in the national economy of Bengal.

BENGALI CULTIVATORS AND THE RESERVE BANK

"In Bengal we ought to take interest in the manner in which French co-operative societies are enabled to finance the cultivators on account of the advances from the *Banque de France*, a topic to which I have been inviting the attention of our countrymen for quite a while. The Reserve Bank should be prevailed upon to cultivate the same relations with our co-operatives and cultivators as the French Central Bank does for those of France.*

SUBSTANTIAL SHARE-CAPITAL FROM BENGALI LOAN OFFICES

"It is time for the directors, managers and others associated with the world of Loan Offices in Bengal to organize measures with a view to secure a substantial portion of Rs. 16,500,000 which is allocated as share-capital for Bengal. Not less than Rs. 5,000,000 should be collectively subscribed by the combined Bengali banks. Here is a chance for the Bengali people to enter "high finance" at the thin end of the wedge, and commence the A.B.C. of functioning on "Indian" economic plat-

*See "The French System of Agricultural Credit" in Sarkar: *Economic Development* (Madras 1926) and his *Law and the Cultivator: The Example of France* in the "Journal of the Bengal National Chamber of Commerce," December 1926.

The convention of 23 June 1928 between the State and the *Banque* may be seen in Lebeau: *La Banque de France* (Paris 1931), pp. 196-198, 321.

forms. There is no more secure method of safeguarding "Bengali interests" in Indian commerce and capitalism than by taking advantage of the provisions offered by the Bill. It is to be trusted that Bengali businessmen will not fail to improve the capital power and financial position of their banks by fresh acquisitions as well as concentrations.

IMPERIAL BANK VIS A VIS RESERVE BANK

"It is curious that the Imperial Bank is to be the only one of the scheduled banks that will enjoy a certain number of gifts from the Reserve Bank. The gifts are the following deposits (Third Schedule Art. 3):

1. Rs. 30,000,000 without interest during the first five years,
2. Rs. 20,000,000 without interest during the next five years,

and so on up to the twenty-fifth year.

"Under the system recommended the Imperial Bank is likely to become a rival of the Reserve Bank to a ertain extent, at any rate, so far as its command over the financial resources is concerned. The proposal that the Imperial Bank should obtain from the Reserve Bank very large amounts as interest-free balances is just calculated almost to introduce a "dyarchy" in Central Banking and ought to be treated as a reactionary and irrational measure. To establish a Reserve Bank and at the same time to continue to bestow certain Central Bank privileges on a private Bank constitute a bankocratic confusion of the worst type,—even although it be for a transitional period. Neither would the *Reichsbank* entertain such a proposition in favour of the *Deutsche Bank und Disconto Gesellschaft*, nor the *Banque de France* for the *Credit Lyonnais*, nor the Bank of England for the Midland.

IMPERIAL BANK VIS A VIS OTHER SCHEDULED BANKS

"In case the Bill in its present form becomes law, the anomalous position of the Imperial Bank in the banking system of India for twenty-five years after the establishment of the Reserve Bank can escape no body's notice. If it is to be a "scheduled bank" i.e., one of the 69 private bnks endowed with the privilege of "signature", on the strength of which the Reserve Bank is authorized to deal in bills of exchange, the Imperial Bank, like all the others, ought to maintain a balance with the Reserve Bank to the extent of 7. 1/2% of the daily average of its demand liabilities *plus* 2. 1/2% of the daily average of its time liabilities [Art. 42 Section (1)]. As a scheduled bank the Imperial Bank should not possess any privileges such as are denied to the others.

"Any preferential treatment of the Imperial Bank is unfair to the other scheduled banks. From their standpoint the proposition is entirely objectionable. The concessions to be enjoyed by the Imperial Bank would spell danger to their normal functioning. As has been pointed out above, they have been relieved of the fear of competition with the Reserve Bank because of statutory safeguards such as serve to curb it of its freedom in functions and delimit the range of its transactions. But out of the frying pan they would be thrown into the fire in so far as they will have to encounter rivalry with the pampered mammoth in the shape of the Imperial Bank, which will be as free as themselves to enter every market.

THE PROPER CONDITIONS OF AGENCY

"The trouble has arisen from the solicitude to entrust the Imperial Bank with the "sole agency" of the Reserve Bank (Third Schedule, Art. 1). The patronage in the form of agencies ought rather to be fairly distributed among a large number of scheduled banks and should not be a monopoly to be enjoyed by just one institution.

"Besides, the period of twenty-five years during which the Imperial Bank is to enjoy the monopoly (Art. 43) should appear to be too long. Businessmen ought to try to have it brought down to not more than seven years.

"There is no reason why the Reserve Bank should fail to develop a large number of branches of its own during the next five or seven years and be as far as possible independent of the Imperial Bank and other scheduled banks in regard to the business that is generally entrusted to agents in the absence of one's own branches."

The Rupee Not Over-valued*

(December 1933)

Interviewed by a representative for an opinion on the recent activities of the Bombay Currency League and the devaluation propaganda Professor Benoy Sarkar said as follows :

"The Rupee is not over-valued in comparison with sterling Devaluation is uncalled for. The eighteenpenny Rupee ought to continue".

FALL IN INDIAN PRICES NOT HEAVIER THAN IN BRITISH

Asked for the reasons for this view Prof. Sarkar observed : "The fall of agricultural prices in India since 1931 cannot be proven to be heavier than that in the United Kingdom. It is perhaps two or three points less. Besides, recent graphs of prices indicate that India's commodities have been tending to firm up. The recovery seems already to be on here and there although in slight proportions."

PRICE-LEVELS: "GENERAL" AND AGRICULTURAL

At this point Prof. Sarkar called special attention to the following points :

"In regard to comparison in price-levels between India and the U.K. it is to be remembered that the Indian "general index" is composed mainly of industrial commodities whereas the British mainly of industrial goods. Comparison in "general price-levels" furnishes no test therefore as to the comparative value of the Rupee *visàvis* sterling. Indeed, scientifically speaking, comparability between the two is eminently questionable because of the fundamental diversity in the structure of the two indices.

* Based on an interview published in the *Ananda Bazar Patrika* (Dec. 2, 1933, *Amrita Bazar Patrika, Forward, Basumati, Hitabadi, Clive Street, Advance* and leading Indian dailies through the news agency, *United Press*, Calcutta.

AGRICULTURAL INDEX LOWER EVERYWHERE

Questioned as to the practical bearing of this situation Prof. Sarkar answered as follows :—

"In countries that are exclusively agricultural or where production and the market are weighted heavily with agricultural goods the price-level has been much more depressed than in industrial countries or those with a greater weightage of manufactured goods. In certain economic regions the discrepancy in the two price-levels has to be measured by not less than 20 per cent during the period of the present depression. The ratio question need not therefore be automatically dragged in simply because a discrepancy of some 5 or 6 points may be detected in the British and the Indian price-levels".

DISCREPANCY: NOMINAL AND REAL

Asked for an opinion as to the real nature of the discrepancy, Professor Sarkar observed :

"While instituting price-comparisons between India and the U.K. one must not be misled into posing the Calcutta or the Bombay index against the British Board of Trade index in its crude form. The investigation will have to be conducted intensively and ought to exihibit the agricultural indices of the two countries in relation to each other. It will be detected that although the fall in the general Board of Trade index is 5 or 6 points more favourable than in the Indian, that in the British agricultural index is perhaps 2 or 3 points less favourable. In other words, for an agricultural country like India the fall in prices happens to be not as heavy as it might otherwise be. In any case, the *real* (as contrasted with nominal) discrepancy in the Indian and British price-levels, should there be any, may turn out to be more in India's favour than in the U.K.'s. The Rupee is perhaps slightly undervalued rather than over-valued. Altogether, the case for devaluation can hardly be made out".

EXPORTS AND PRICES INDIFFERENT TO RATIO

On the general problem of raising prices Prof. Sarkar said :—

"It is not enough to speculate in season and out of season on the alleged stimulation of exports or raising of prices by currency depreciation. Statistical realities have also to be faced in the most objective and open-eyed manner. Factually, the exports from India increased even under a 'high' Rupee (1s. 6d.). The export-curves previous to 1929 were not influenced by exchange-curves in the manner as expected according to theory. And at the present moment it is worth while to observe, further, that price-curves in India are likewise indifferent to the course of currency. Prices rose in the past even with a relatively high Rupee as established in 1927. They may rise again, as indeed they have been tending to rise, under the same ratio. A change in the *status quo* of exchange is therefore unnecessary."

PROSPERITY ALREADY IN EVIDENCE

About the present export situation of India Professor Sarkar said: "The period of six months from April to September 1933 bespeaks a more prosperous half-year than the coresponding period of 1932. For instance, the exports of both raw cotton and raw jute have considerably improved and the price of cotton has been looking up. Prosperity is already in evidence, albeit no doubt only in traces."

WANTED CAPITAL IMPORTS

Asked as to the prospects of a more substantial rise in Indian prices Professor Sarkar replied as follows:—

"There is every likelihood of American, British and French capital being exported to agricultural countries and other normally capital-borrowing regions. As soon as these capital movements which have been very little in evidence since 1929 resume their usual course the agricultural produce and raw materials of debtor countries like India may be expected to be placed finally on their pathway upward, as indeed they were previous to the world-depression in the epoch of more or less free capital movements."

BENEFICIAL TO AGRICULTURISTS

Prof. Sarkar was in favour of 1s. 6d. in the curency controversy of 1926-27. In 1931 he supported Rupee-Sterling linking. The Ottawa Agreement was likewise supported by him last year (1932). All these measures have in his judgment been beneficial to Indian agriculturists and exports from India. On the question of the Reserve Bank his views are already wellknown as being in general agreement with the provisions of the Bill.

CHART 1

American and British Investments Abroad
(1919-32)

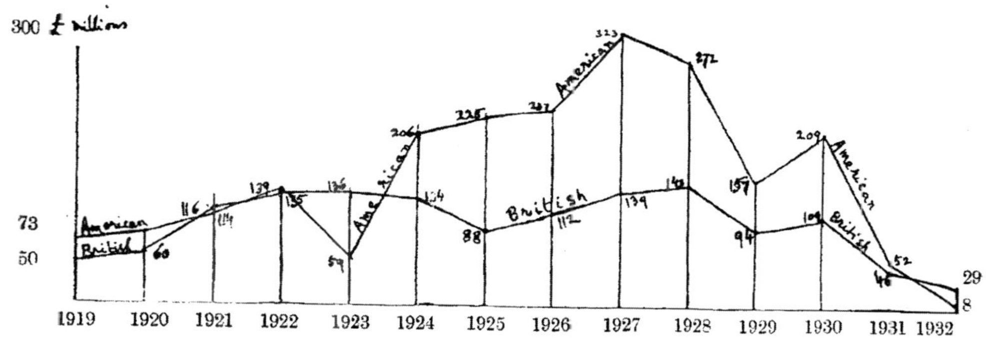

(To face page 39)

Price-Curves in the Perspective of Exchange-Curves

(December 1933)

I. FORECASTING THE RECOVERY

In the paper on "Economic Planning for Bengal" published in the *Insurance and Finance Review* for March 1933 the present writer was in a position to make the following observations: "By the next autumn (i.e. September-October 1933) we may expect the definite beginnings of a new situation, the world-recovery being in sight. It is within a year afterwards i.e. about the Pujah season of 1934 that the cultivators and Zamindars of Bengal may hope to experience the solid effects of recovery."

One of the processes involved in this recovery was considered to be the "removal of the friction that is hindering the smooth export and import of capital". The beginning of the depression in 1929 was visualized as consisting to a considerable extent in the reduction of capital movements. Thus, "the U.S.A., Great Britain, France, Canada, Czechoslovakia and Sweden which together exported 2,174,000 dollars in 1928 could export so little as 891,000,000 dollars in 1929. Since then they have become more shy. On the other hand, Germany, Australia, Poland, Argentina, Hungary, India, Finland and Norway, which together borrowed 1,736,000,000 dollars in 1928 could borrow barely 1,000,000,000 dollars in 1929. Our own country, for instance, was almost starved financially, investments in India being reduced from 67 million to 36 million dollars."[1]

(See Chart I)

The question of recovery was subsequently discussed by the present author in "The Seven Years of *Arthik Unnati*" in the economic monthly *Arthik Unnati* (Economic Progress) for April-May 1933 in the following manner: "One of the means to the expansion of the exports and

1 *Compte rendu de la Banque de France* (Paris 1933), pp. 57; *Federal Reserve Bulletin* (Washington, November 1932), p. 698; *The Course and Phases of the World Economic Depression* (Geneva 1931), pp. 20, 06, 201, 203; *Midland Bank Monthly Review* (London), January-February 1933.

imports of goods consists in the arrangements for the expansion of exports and imports of capital. For several years British and American finance has been reaching the world's markets in diminished doses. Most of the countries of the world considerably depend on foreign capital for the promotion of their agriculture, industry and commerce. India is one of them. The import of capital implies that the import of foreign goods is being facilitated. The consequence will naturally be the quickening of industrial activity in the capital-lending countries and hence a reduction in unemployment. On the other hand, in order to pay for the machineries and other goods imported as well as for the interest of foreign capital the exports will tend to rise from capital-borrowing countries. And this will lead to prosperity among cultivators as well as Zamindars.

"It is after the World-Economic Conference to be held in London during the next summer that Anglo-American capital will commence to move in the normal directions. In that case the Eur-American depression will begin to pass away in the course of this very year. And so far as India is concerned we may expect to see some of the pre-depression conditions in the Pujah season, if not already in the summer, of the next year. What is wanted in Bengal is foreign capital."

The subject was pursued further in September 1933 in the course of the present author's address at Mymensingh as President of the Bengali People's Literary Conference. The problem of the Bengali cultivator was touched upon in the context of world-recovery as follows: "The price of jute has not yet risen. But it seems to me that it will not fail to rise in the near future. Opportunities are being created abroad for the sale of Bengal jute. The Sei-Yu-Kai Party of Japan has after the election of 1932 instituted a "five-year plan" with capital worth 400,000,000 Yens in order to stimulate manufacturing industries and encourage productive enterprises. With the commencement of movements in Japanese economic life the demand for foreign goods is bound to rise in Japan. As soon as Hitler became Chancellor in Germany in January 1933 he set on foot the campagin against unemployment and his enterprises are to involve a total outlay of 1,000,000,000 Reichsmarks. The economic developments of Germany are likewise expected to lead to the increase of German demand for foreign goods. In April (1933) President Roosevelt has begun revivifying the American markets with redoubled enthusiasm. The enhancement of American prices can have but a salutary repercussion on the world-economy. And the Government of the United Kingdom is likewise active in carrying through measures of economic policy such as are calculated to stimulate exports and raise agricultural prices.

"In many countries the Governments are up and doing in order to combat economic stagnation and promote prosperity. The demand for exports from Bengal cannot but rise on account of these intensifications of economic activities abroad. The peasants and planters of Bengal will thereby be furnished with chances to export relatively greater quantities of jute, tea, etc. On the other hand, the Railway Companies of India are going to be furnished with the authority to run buses and motors. This will automatically stimulate road construction in the districts. Besides, as soon as the question of reconstructing the Howrah Bridge is taken up at Calcutta a new era is likely to dawn in the import of iron, steel, hardware, cement, petrol, motor, electric apparatus and installations etc. In order to buy all these foreign goods it will be necessary for Bengal to export larger quantities of jute. Finally, there is the rise in the price of silver to be taken into account. As a result the liquidity of cash in the hands of our countrymen is likely to rise. This also can but serve to raise the price of jute. When all these items are considered together it should appear that after April or by September-October, i.e., the Pujah season of 1934 the condition of the jute cultivators will be marked by signs of relative prosperity. And the receipts of rent by the Zamindars also will augment in value."

II. EXPANSION OF EXPORTS

1. *Signs of Recovery in India*

It is possible to-day to make a retrospective survey of the last few months on a statistical basis.

The Indian official year 1933-34 may be said to have commenced with marks of recovery. Let us watch the recent fortunes of an important commodity, namely, raw jute.

During the week ending December 9, 1933 [2] the total arrivals of jute into Calcutta were numbered at 253,000 bales of 400 lbs. each as against 210,000 bales of the corresponding week in the previous year. From July 1 to December 9, 1933 the total arrivals were numbered at 5,267,000 bales as against 4,615,000 bales of the corresponding period in 1932. From August to October the total exports amounted 135,000 tons in 1931, 137,000 tons in 1932 and 165,000 tons in 1933. On all counts it is thus possible to note an increase.

2 *Indian Trade Journal* (Calcutta) Dec. 14, 1933 pp. 898-99.

For November the jute exports have expanded in the following manner :—

1931	...	...	576,895 bales of 400 lbs. each
1932	...	...	362,398 ,, ,, ,, ,,
1933	...	...	623,760 ,, ,, ,, ,,

Let us now pass on to the total exports.

The trend of export from India during the seven half-years from April 1930 to September 1933 is indicated below :—[3]

1930 April-September	Rs. 1,251,300,000
1930-31 October-March	,, 1,005,100,000
1931: April-September	,, 780,100,000
1931-32 October-March	,, 825,300,000
1932 April-September	,, 621,900,000
1932-33 : October-March	,, 734,400,000
1933 April-September	,, 726,900,000

(See Chart II)

In order to understand these figures properly it would be necessary to take the busy seasons (October-March) together and separate them from the slack season (April-September). It is to be observed that the exports for Oct.-March 1932-33 are lower than those for Oct.-March 1931-32, and these again from those for Oct.-March 1930-31. In other words, during these three years (1930-33) the busy season did not know any trace of revival. The decline was continuous.

As regards the slack season,—down to April-September 1932 the decline was likewise steady and continuous during the period of three years from April 1930. But for the first time in April-September 1933 it is possible to mark a slight ascent in the curve from Rs. 621,900,000 to Rs. 726,900,000.

The tendency is upward. And this is verified also by the figure for the next month. Thus the four October exports were as follows :

1930	...	...	...	Rs. 181,400,000
1931	...	...	...	,, 131,100,000
1932	...	...	...	,, 117,600,000
1933	...	...	...	,, 129,100,000

Here, again, the story is one of a rise in reference to the previous year, although of course the figure is still below those for 1931 and 1930.

3 *Indian Finance* (Calcutta) for November 18, 1933 and December 9, 1933. Based on *Accounts Relating to the Seaborne Trade and Navigation of British India* (Delhi) for September 1932 and 1933.

CHART 2

The Exports, Imports and Trade Balance of India
(April 1930-September 1933)

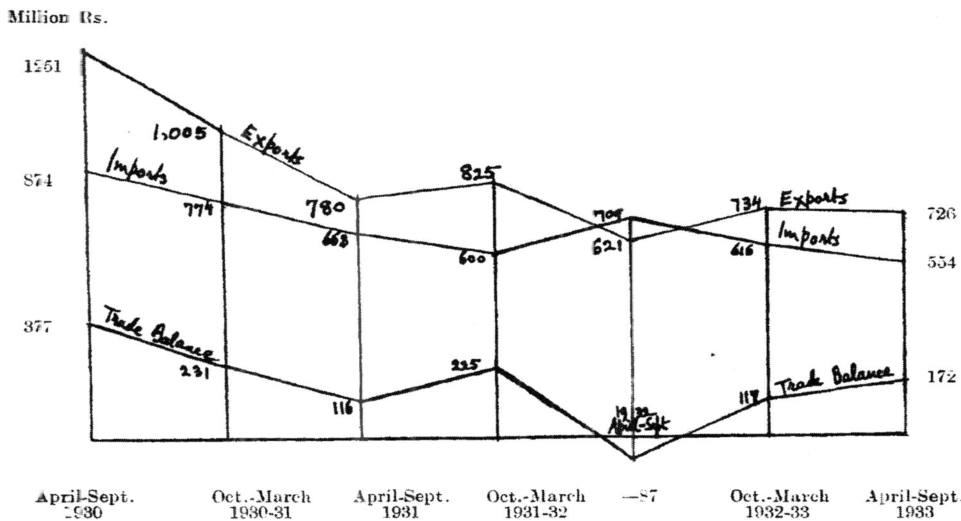

(To face page 42)

2. *Recovery in World-Economy*

We shall now examine the business conditions prevailing abroad.

The exports of France during the first ten months of 1933 totalled 2,588,000,000 t, in weight as against 2,257,000,000 t, of the corresponding period of 1932.[4]

In Italy[5] unemployment was registered at 907,463 on September 30, 1933 as against 949,408 of the corresponding date in the previous year. Industrial production during the period January to September 1933 was in the majority of instances higher than in the previous year. The increment was in certain instances as high as 60 per cent, and in any case more than 30 per cent in a large number of cases.

Unemployment went down in Germany[6] from 6,013,612 in January 1933 to 4,856,000 in June 1933. By November 1933 the unemployed list was brought down to 3,700,000. The number was 30 per cent lower than that in November 1932.

Numerous industries have been exhibiting signs of increase in the volume of production. In August 1933 the industrial consumption of electricity was 14 per cent higher than in 1932. The goods traffic on railways points likewise to the direction of a quickening of business.

The excess of exports over imports in October was registered at 100,000,000 Reichsmarks.

By September 1933 substantial and sustained improvement was noticeable in the British economic charts.[7] The curve of employment indicated an encouraging rise. The volume of industrial production was at a higher level than a year or two ago and was spread over a wide range of industries. Country and provincial bank clearings revealed a distinct upward trend. Import curves were not unsatisfactory. Considerable expansion was noticeable in the home market and this was associated with a distinct upward movement in commodity values.

4 *Journal du Commerce* (Paris) Nov. 15, 1933.

5 *Rassegna Economica* (Naples) for October 1933, p. 534. Mario Vergottini: "Gli Indici del Movimento economico Italiano" in *La Vita Economica Italiana* (Rome) for October 1933, pp. 4. 10-14, 19, 21.

6 *World Economic Survey 1932-33* (Geneva 1933) p. 326; Sarkar: "The Hitler-State" in the *Insurance and Finance Review* (Calcutta) for October-November 1933.

Deutsche Bank und Disconto Gesellschaft Wirtschaftliche Mitteilungen (Berlin, 21 Nov. 1933) pp. 200-208. See also *Technik und Wirtschaft* (Berlin, December 1933): *Die deutsche Wirtschaft Mitte November* 1933, Ten Charts on pp. 369-371.

7 *Midland Bank Monthly Review* (London) August-September, 1933, pp. 4-7.

By June 1933 the value of Australian exports was well above the level of a year ago. This was the position in New Zealand also.[8]

In August 1933 the index number of Canadian business was 89·8 as against 78·1 of twelve months ago. Unemployment had been declining progressively.

In Sweden industrial production and employment in November 1933 were above the level of a year ago. The statistics of shipping industry indicated improvements both in Norway and Denmark.

With 1923-25 = 100 the index of U.S. industrial production in manufactures[9] rose from 59 in August 1932 to 91 in August 1933, and in minerals from 65 to 91. Likewise did the total factory employment rise from 58·8 to 73·3 and factory pay rolls from 40·1 to 55·7.

With 1928 = 100 the index of industrial production in certain countries is exhibited for January and June 1933 in the perspective of the corresponding months of 1932 as follows:[10]

	January		June.	
	1932	1933	1932	1933
Germany	62	62	61	70
Austria	72	61	63	64 (May)
Belgium	72	72	63	75
Canada	68	53	65	68
U.S.A.	65	59	53	80
France	83	79	73	88
Japan	96	117	104	131 (June)
Poland	52	47	54	58
U.K.	90	89	89	89
	(1st quarter)	(1st qr.)		
Sweden	93	84	77	82

With the exception of Japan the index for January 1933 was lower in every country indicated above than that for January 1932. But from June 1932 to June 1933 the story is one of universal rise with the exception of the U.K., where the index is constant.

3. *Comparative Depths of Depression*

It is perhaps appropriate at this stage to survey the depths of depression in India and abroad with special reference to exports. The examination will furnish us not only with a comparative estimate of the

8 "Business Recovery in the Sterling Group" in the *Midland Bank Monthly Review* for October-November 1933, pp. 2-3.

9 *Federal Reserve Bulletin* for October 1933, pp. 662-664.

10 *World Economic Survey* 1932-33, p. 325.

diversities between the different countries but also with an idea of the relative recovery achieved up till now or at all possible in each economic region.

The depth of the depression in India can be felt in the following figures of total trade (both imports and exports). From Rs. 5,687,000,000 in 1929-30 it fell to 2,710,800,000 in 1932-33.[11] With 1929-30 as 100 the index in 1932-33 was 47·6.

For the purposes of international comparison all recorded values may be reduced to dollars.[12] Judged by a uniform standard India's position in 1932 is found to be much lower than 47·6.

With 1929 as 100 the total world-trade (imports and exports combined) was 38·8 in 1932. India's position was 34·0 i.e. lower than the world's general level. And in this she was not in spendid isolation. It is possible to mention at least the following countries, the index of whose total trade like that of India fell lower than the world trade index :—

World-Trade	38·8
Germany	38·5
Canada	35·1
Australia	35·0
China	34·6
India	34·0
Argentine	31·5
U.S.A.	30·6

The fall in Argentina and the U.S.A. was deeper than in India. The position of Canada and Australia was slightly higher than that of India. The United Kingdom with 39·8 was not much above the world-trade level. In any case, the discrepancy between India and the U.K. was to be measured by not more than 5·8 points.

India's percentage of the world's trade (in imports and exports combined) went down from 3·2 per cent in 1929 to 2·65 per cent in 1932.[13] The decrease was due to the diminution of exports. In this phenomenon India had comrades in the U.S.A. with the story of decline from 13·83 to 10·92, in Canada (3·68 to 3·33), Germany (9·34 to 9·29), Argentina (2·52 to 2·05), China (2·13 to 1·90), Australia (1·89 to 1·71), Czechoslovakia (1·74 to 1·65), Dutch East Indies (1·50 to 1·47), Spain (1.36 to 1·24), Brazil (1·29 to 1·07), British Malaya (1·48 to 1·07), Austria (1·12 to 0·94), Poland (0·97 to 0·82), New Zealand (0·72 to 0·70), Egypt (0·76 to 0·70), Mexico (0·68 to 0·60), Cuba (0·71 to 0·52), Finland (0·49 to 0·47),

11 *Review of the Trade of India* in 1932-33 (Delhi 1933), p. 158.

12 *Review of World Trade* 1932 (Geneva 1933) p. 29.

13 *Review of World Trade* 1932 (Geneva 1933) p. 27.

Hungary (0·53 to 0·44), Jugoslovia (0·39 to 0·37), Chile (0·70 to 0·26), Persia (0·30 to 0·25), Greece (0·38 to 0·24), French Indo-China (0·30 to 0·24), Peru (0·30 to 0·21), Uruguay (0·27 to 0·20), Nigeria (0·22 to 0·17), French West Africa (0·16 to 0·14), Latvia (0·18 to 0·13), Kenya (0·11 to 0·10), Bolivia (0·11 to 0·08), Esthonia (0·09 to 0·08), and Gautemala (0·08 to 0·06).

Relatively speaking, the exports of India should not appear to have declined more disastrously than those of many other countries.

At 1932[14] the percentage decline in exports since 1929 may be seen for certain countries as below :—

	A			Countries.	Percent
	Countries	Percent.	9.	Jugoslavia:	64
1.	Denmark:	53		Egypt:	64
	Belgium:	53		Sweden:	64
2.	Australia:	55		United Kingdom:	64
	Finland:	55		Czechoslovakia:	64
3.	Netherlands:	57		Argentine:	64
	Italy:	57	10.	Mexico:	65
4.	New Zealand:	58		Spain:	65
	Germany:	58	11.	Peru:	67
	B		12.	Hungary:	68
5.	Irish Free State:	60	13.	U.S.A.:	69
	Japan:	60	14.	India:	70
	Canada:	60		C	
6.	Brazil:	61	15.	Austria:	71
	Greece:	61		Uruguay:	71
	France:	61	16.	China:	75
7.	Poland:	62		British Malaya:	75
8.	Switzerland:	63	17.	Chile:	84

Nearly three dozen countries sustained a decline in exports exceeding 50 per cent in the course of four years. In five countries, namely, Chile, British Malaya, China, Uruguay and Austria the decline was heavier than in India and ranged between 71 and 84 per cent. India's position which is measured by a decline of 70 per cent was almost identical with that of the U.S.A. (69%) and Hungary (68%). Six countries, namely, Argentina, Czechoslovakia, U.K., Sweden, Egypt and Jugoslavia, each with a decline of 64 per cent, happened to be just a few points ahead of India. Nay, all those countries which are marked by a decline down to 60 per cent, namely, Irish Free State (60%), Japan (60%), Canada (60%), Brazil (61%), France (61%), Poland (62%), and Switzerland (63%) might be described as belonging almost to the same fraternity of adversity as Hungary, U.S.A., India and Austria.

14 *World Economic Survey 1932-33* (Geneva 1933) p. 214.

The demand for Indian goods in foreign countries was less keen than that of India for foreign goods. This is, first, a function of agricultural economy, and secondly, a function of debtor-economy. Hence the decline in the percentage of exports was heavier than that in the percentage of imports.

The relative decline in India's exports and imports may be seen as follows:[15]

	Value		Indices	
	1929-30	1932-33	1929-30	1932-33
	Rs.			
Exports	3,108,000,000.	1,324,100,000	100	42·4
Imports	2,389,500,000.	1,322,700,000	100	55·2

The decline in exports was 57·6 per cent while that in imports 44·8 per cent.

It is to be observed that in India as in other agricultural countries[16] it is not so much the quantum of exports as their prices that fell,—as we shall have occasion to discuss at length in a subsequent section. On the other hand, in regard to the industrial goods imported by India it is not so much the prices as the quantum that fell. That is, India obtained relatively fewer Rupees but had to pay relatively more Rupees. Hence the discrepancy in the rates of decline bearing on imports and exports with its natural consequence on the trade balance.

The decline in India's balance of trade in merchandise since 1929 can be seen as follows:[17]

Pre-war average:	Rs. 782,700,000
War average:	,, 763,100,000
1928-29:	,, 864,700,000
1929-30:	,, 789,800,000
1930-31:	,, 620,500,000
1931-32:	,, 348,300,000
1932-33:	,, 33,600,000

A heavy fall in the balance of trade, i.e. in the decline of export surplus, is inevitable in agricultural countries whose exports are less in demand abroad but whose demands for foreign goods continue to be keen, and for one reason or other have not been controlled or

15 *Review of the Trade of India in 1932-33* p. 153.

16 *Review of the Trade of India in 1932-33* p. 153. See also *Supra*, pp. 20-23.

17 *World Production and Prices* 1925-32 (Geneva, 1933), p. 14, 104-110. See also Appendix III, Tables 3-7.

restricted by legislative action. The alleged "favourable balance" of India in pre-depression years is but a function of all debtor countries which have to pay the creditors abroad in export. Similarly, creditor countries like the U.K., France, Netherlands and Switzerland have normally "unfavourable" balance.[18]

Economically, therefore, the category, favourable or unfavourable, as applied to the balance of trade does not possess any substantial significance, especially from the standpoint of prosperity or the reverse. For instance, in 1930 the balance was unfavourable for the U.K., France, Italy, Belgium and Switzerland. On the contrary, it was favourable for Germany, Poland, Rumania, Hungary and Bulgaria. It was not, however, the group with a favourable balance that was the more prosperous, as points out Mons. Julien Durand.[19]

All the same, it is worth while to observe that the trade balance of India has been improving, as will be evident in the following statement of export surplus from April 1930 to September 1933 :—

		Exports Rs.	Imports Rs.	Export-Surplus Rs.
1930.	April-Sept.	1,251,300,000	874,100,000	+377,200,000
1930-31.	Oct-March	1,005,100,000	774,100,000	+231,000,000
1931.	April-Sept.	780,100,000	663,500,000	+116,600,000
1931-32.	Oct-March	825,300,000	600,200,000	+225,100,000
1932.	April-Sept.	621,900,000	709,000,000	−87,100,000
1932-33.	Oct-March	734,400,000	616,800,000	+117,600,000
1933.	April-Sept.	726,900,000	554,800,000	+172,100,000

The trade balance of the latest slack season (April-September 1933) was larger than that of the preceding busy season (1932-33, October-March). The improvement should appear to be remarkable in view of the fact that the corresponding slack season of 1932 was marked by a negative figure, imports exceeding exports. That half-year represented indeed the nadir of depression in the Indian economy. As it is, the latest figure (Rs. 172,100,000) is considerably above that of the corresponding season of two years ago (Rs. 116,600,000). This is another symptom along with the others already indicated that India is perhaps fairly *en route* to recovery.

18 *Review of World Trade* 1932 (Geneva 1933) pp. 57-59; *World Economic Survey 1932-33*, pp. 287-289.

19 "Le Commerce Exterieur de la France" in *Journal du Commerce* (Paris) for November 1933.

CHART 3

Exports of Raw Cotton in Quantum and Value as well as Prices Per Ton Exported

(April 1931-September 1933)

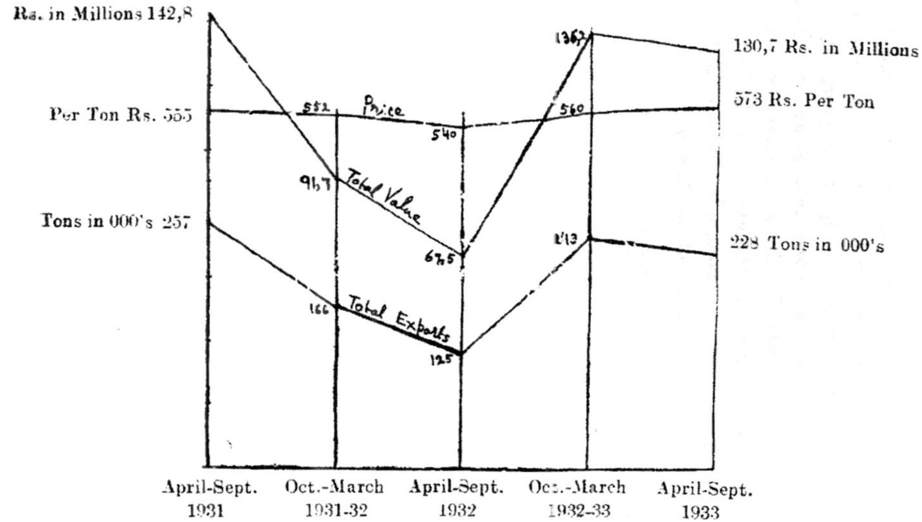

(To face page 49)

4. *The Behaviour of Cotton, Jute, and Oil Seeds on the Export Market*

If we examine the behaviour of some of the exported staples we find the individual trends to be in the main of the same character as the general trend of the whole export movement. Let us take the three commodities, raw cotton, oil seeds, and raw jute, for this analysis.

The story of the exports of raw cotton, oil seeds and raw jute during the five half-years from April 1931 to September 1933 is as follows (in 000 tons):—

Half-years	Raw Cotton	Oil Seeds	Raw Jute
1931 April-Sept	257	491	234
1931-32 Oct-March	166	497	353
1932 April-Sept.	125	298	190
1932-33. Oct-March	243	434	373
1933 April-Sept.	228	576	305

The quantum curve for raw cotton yields the following equations:

1. April-Sept. 1933 (228) = 1·82 April-Sept. 1932 (125)
2. Oct.-March 1932-33 (243) = 1·46 Oct.-March 1931-32 (166)

The latest slack season exhibits a great improvement (1·82 times) upon the previous one. The latest busy season was likewise an improvement (1·46 times) upon the corresponding season of 1931-32. The periods from April 1931 to September 1932 marked the different phases of continuous decline in exports. As against the fall, steep as it is, from 257,000 tons to 125,000 tons the ascent from April 1932 to September 1933, although not continuous, is remarkable. Compared to April-September 1932 the expansion of cotton exports in April-September 1933 bespeaks a year and a half of relative but substantiel prosperity. It may not be out of place to notice that the latter part of this period almost coincides with the first trade year under the Ottawa Agreement.

(See Chart III)

No less interesting is it to record that during the earlier part of this period which coincides with the suspension of the gold-standard (from October-March 1932-33 to April-September 1932) the curve is one of decline. The currency depression failed to arrest the decline.

For oil-seeds the quantum-curve presents a somewhat different shape. We have the following equation:

April-Sept. 1933 (576) = 1·9 April-Sept. 1932 (298).

During the recent slack season the exports have almost doubled themselves in comparison with the corresponding season of the previous year.

But the busy season of October-March 1932-33 was still less prosperous than the busy season of 1931-32.

The most important feature, however, consists in the fact that the exports (576,000 tons) during the slack season of 1933 have exceeded those of the busy season (October-March) of 1931-32 as well as those of the slack season of 1931. The result is a steep rise from the depth of April-September 1932. This is to be contrasted with the break in the quantum curve of raw cotton during the same period.

The behaviour of oil seeds has been different from that of raw cotton in another important regard. In the *milieu* of the suspension of the gold standard raw cotton did not experience an expansion, but rather went headlong down. Under the same circumstances, however, oil seeds experienced a slight rise. But in any case the expansion was ephemeral. By April-September 1932 oil seeds and raw cotton found themselves as bed-fellows in a more or less common trough. That trough must, however, be treated as, relatively speaking, normal since it is the regular slack season.

(See Chart IV)

For the nearest slack and busy seasons the equations furnished by the quantum curve of raw jute are similar to, if not identical with, those furnished by that of raw cotton. There is noticeable an expansion in both these seasons. Thus

1. April-Sept. 1933 (305) = 1·6 April-Sept. 1932 (190)
2. Oct.-March 1932-33 (373) = 1·05 Oct.-March 1931-32 (353)

The quantum of jute exports during April-September 1933 is 1·6 times that during the corresponding season of the preceding year. In comparison with the cotton curve the rise in the jute curve is somewhat low. In regard to the active season also the rise is much lower for jute than for cotton. Altogether, although jute like cotton has been substantially on the upward trend in exports its equations are not relatively as satisfactory as those of the latter. Neither jute nor cotton has of course experienced during the period in question the same amount of expansion as the oil seeds. There is a difference in the rates of expansion; but all the three commodities have one story to tell,—that of increased exports since the nadir of April-September 1932.

The recent story of jute is identical with that of cotton in so far as the rising curve encounters a break. This break is but natural since the peak of the busy season (October-March 1932) can hardly be maintained in the succeeding slack season. Thus considered, the fortunes of oil seeds have turned out to be rather unusually favourable at the present moment.

CHART 4

Exports of Oilseeds in Quantum and Value as well as Prices Per Ton Exported
(April 1931-September 1933)

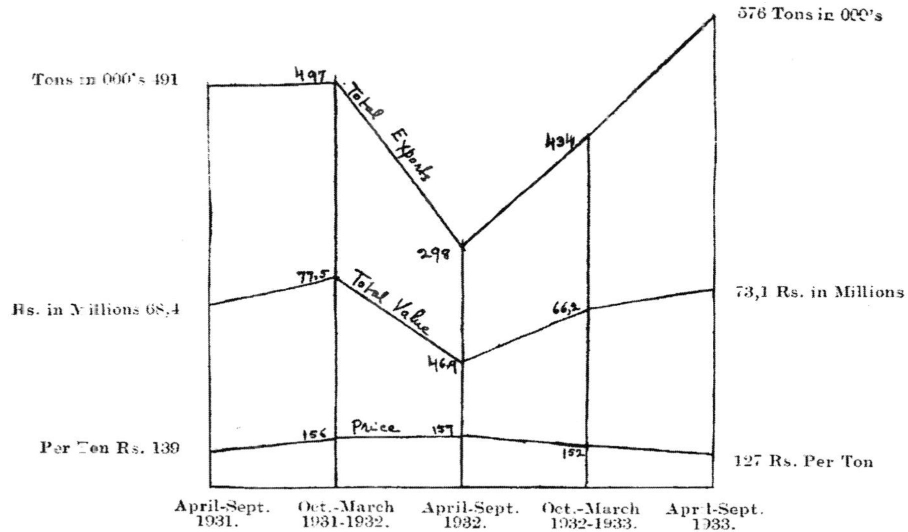

(To face page 50)

CHART 5

Exports of Raw Jute in Quantum and Value as well as Prices Per Ton Exported
(April 1931-September 1933)

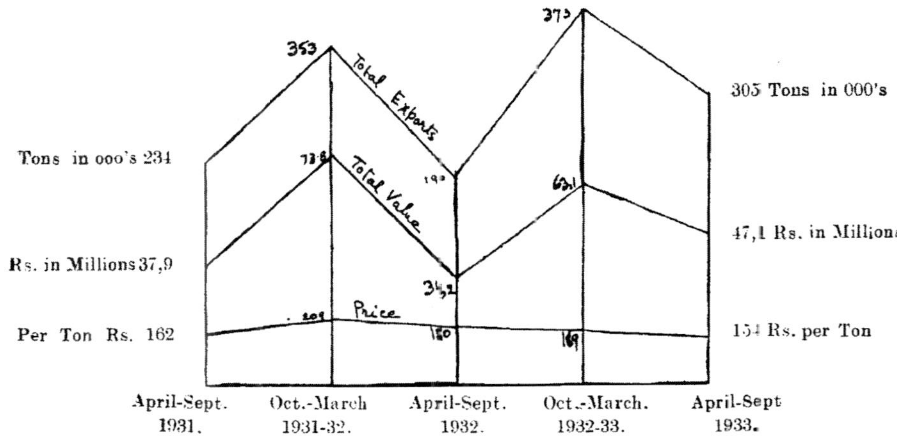

(To face page 5?)

(See Chart V)

From September 1932 to September 1933 we have to orient ourselves chiefly to the background of the first Ottawa year. The expansion of exports in raw cotton, oil-seeds and raw jute, although at different rates, is a striking fact of this *milieu*.

But certain differences are to be watched in the relations between the three commodities for the period from April 1931 to September 1932. The suspension of the gold standard was the special feature of that period. Both jute and oil seeds reacted favourably under that impulse, although again, at different rates; but the responses of cotton were definitely negative, as we have seen above. In the case of jute the peak of October-March 1931-32 (353,000 tons) was exceeded by that of 1932-33 (373,000 tons). This, however, was not the case with the curve of oil-seeds. But the position at September 1933 is more or less identical for oil seeds and jute in so far as both exhibit a peak higher than the corresponding peak not only of 1932 but also of 1931.

III. THE ECONOMICS OF COMPARATIVE INDUSTRIALISM

1. *Discrepancies in Depression and Recovery*

Like all other economic phenomena depression and recovery affect different countries in different ways, and with diverse degrees of intensity. Neither the depth of depression nor the height of recovery,—even under conditions of universal economic transformation,—is to be taken as a uniform category. Discrepancies in recovery as well as in depression are to be treated as a matter of course.

The regions which happen to be thrown together politically, for instance, in the British Commonwealth of Nations or in the French Empire do not by virtue of this legal and administrative nexus possess any economic traits such as are likely to render them uniformly susceptible to the same sets of world-forces. Similarly, there may not exist any really basic bonds of uniformity between a certain number of countries which for some definite periods or purposes may happen to follow the same currency or tariff policies. In each of these instances of Imperial unity or federation as well as tariff unions and currency blocs there may exist often or once in a while relations of mutual economic dependence under which the regions perhaps supplement one another from various points of view. But even this economic interdependence cannot by itself engender in them a unifrom behaviour *vis-à-vis* a fall or rise in prices or an expansion or contraction of trade movements.

The validity of alleged universal economic laws like the quantitative theory of money, the purchasing power parity doctrine etc., is limited by these considerations about the factual diversity of the spheres in which the economic forces operate. Reactions of exactly equal magnitudes are by the nature of the case but rare accidents in regions or fields ostensibly subject to the play of mathematically equal doses of a certain economic influence.

It is well established that in the national economy of a single community not all the classes or groups of persons are equally or uniformly affected by a tariff, price-change or taxation etc. Each is influenced according to its own economic status and financial staying-power. It is to be understood likewise that in the world-economy no two regions are likely to be influenced in one and the same manner by the same complex of agencies. The influence will depend on the economic *locus standi* of the regions concerned. Diversity or discrepancy is a profound reality of comparative industrialism or an international study of the world's diverse economic regions. The comparability of magnitudes derived from diverse fields i.e. of the international statistical data is thereby rendered almost invariably open to question.

2. *Agricultural vs. Industrial Countries*

The most fundamental consideration in the economic behaviour of a region is furnished by its economic structure. The reactions to world-economic forces to which it is likely to be prone are in the last analysis dependent on the number, character and strength of its producers and consumers. It is in the active economic agents, the effective professional groups, the nature, diversity and variety of the occupations that the real sources of a region's economic behaviour are to be found.

The categories, "agricultural country," "industrial country," or "agrar-industrial country," are likely to be misleading unless each one is defined with special reference to the proportion of "actives" or the "gainfully employed" in relation to the total population. To be concrete, let us start to ascertain exactly which country or countries on the surface of the earth may be regarded as India's comrades in comparative industrialism or international economic statistics.

From the standpoint of the proportion of persons employed in agriculture[20] in percentage of total population we can divide some thirty-one countries of the world into the following three groups:

A.

Above 25% of Total Population

1	Lithuania:	47·6	7	Finland:	33·2
2	Bulgaria:	44·0	8	India:	33·1
3	Russia:	41·6	9	Hungary:	26·9
4	Rumania:	40·6	10	Italy:	26·5
5	Poland:	39·9	11	Portugal:	26·2
6	Esthonia:	37·0			

B

Between 10 and 25% of Total Population

1	France:	23·2	8	Germany:	15·6
2	Mexico:	23·2	9	Norway:	14·8
3	Austria:	22·0	10	Denmark:	14·5
4	Spain:	21·0	11	Chile:	14·0
5	Sweden:	17·9	12	Canada:	12·6
6	Czechoslovakia:	17·8	13	Switzerland:	12·4
7	Greece:	16·8	14	U. S. A.:	10·3

C.

Under 10% of Total Population

1	Austria:	9·6	4	Belgium:	8·3
2	Holland:	9·2	5	Argentine:	6·7
3	New Zealand:	9·1	6	England-Wales:	3·4

So far as the economic structure of India, as based on the agricultural profession, is concerned, her nearest neighbours or comrades are Portugal, Italy, Hungary, Finland, Esthonia, Poland and Rumania.

In regard to the persons employed in industry and mining in percentage of total population, the same thirty-one countries may be clssified in the following three groups:

A.

Above 15% of Total Population

1	England-Wales:	24·0	5	Austria:	18·3
2	Germany:	21·0	6	France:	18·0
3	Switzerland:	20·0	7	Holland:	15·0
4	Belgium:	19·0			

20 *Statistisches Jahrbuch für das Deutsche Reich 1928* (Berlin) pp. 26*-27*, *Annuaire Statistique International* 1928 (Geneva) pp. 42-43; Woytinsky; *Die Welt in Zahlen* (Berlin 1927) Vol. I p. 57. *Statistical Abstract for British India 1920-1930* (Calcutta 1932), pp. 36-37; *Statistique Generale de la France Annuaire Statistique 1931* (Paris 1931), pp. 214*-215*.

B.

Between 5% and 15% of Total Population

1	Australia:	14·7	9	Argentine:	10·0
2	Czechoslovakia:	14·0	10	New Zealand:	9·8
3	Swedon:	13·0	11	Chile:	9·0
4	U. S. A.:	13·0	12	Canada:	8·9
5	Italy:	13·0	13	Hungary:	8·0
6	Finland:	12·0	14	Denmark:	7·5
7	Norway:	11·8	15	Esthonia:	7·5
8	Portugal:	10·0			

C.

Under 5% of Total Population

1	India:	5.0	6	Bulgaria:	4·0
2	Spain:	5·0	7	Mexico:	4·0
3	Greece:	5·0	8	Russia:	4·0
4	Poland:	5·0	9	Lithuania:	3·7
5	Rumania:	4·0			

Industrially considered, the economic structure of India bears the closest affinity to Lithuania, Russia, Mexico, Bulgaria, Rumania, Poland, Greece, Spain, Esthonia and Denmark. Should those countries from the agricultural group be singled out which happen also to belong to this group one may believe that perhaps the real economic peers of India have been brought together. Under these considerations, it is Rumania, Poland and Esthonia, as well as Bulgaria, Lithuania and Russia,—these six countries that should be regarded as akin and comparable to Indian economic morphology.[21] If, then, these seven countries be taken as representing the types of "agricultural regions," most of the countries which in general parlance even among economists and statistical specialists pass for agricultural countries, must be considered to be lying outside the agricultural sphere. The impacts of general economic forces on these countries—their demands for diverse categories of goods, their purchasing power, their price-levels etc.—are not likely to be the same in nature and extent as those on the seven agricultural regions.

There is no doubt that England-Wales, Germany, Holland and U.S.A., are "industrial' countries. It is necessary also to observe that compared to India and her six comrades not only Norway and Italy but also Argentine, New Zealand, Canada and Hungary belong to the "industrial group." "To come nearer home," Australia, Canada, and New Zealand, are not substantially akin to India in agricultural economy, as is generally surmised not only in India but also abroad even in statistically equipped and official circles.

21 Sarkar: *Economic Development* (Madras 1926), pp. 127, 303; *Applied Economics* Vol. I. (Calcutta 1939), pp. 89-95, 148-153, 292, 297-98,

3. *Debtor vs. Creditor Countries*

Like the professional character of the "actives" the character of the region as capital-borrowing or capital-lending is a most important item in its economic structure. And it is very interesting to observe that during 1922-31 only the following were creditor countries :—

1 United Kingdom
2 United States or America
3 France
4 Netherlands
5 Switzerland
6 Irish Free State
7 Sweden.

Practically all the other countries of the world, agricultural, industrial or agrar-industrial, are debtor countries. India at any rate is one such country, having had to pay abroad the following amounts (in dollars) from 1923 to 1931.[22]

1923-24	:	99,100,000	1927-28	:	114,700,000
1924-25	:	105,500,000	1928-29	:	118,600,000
1925-26	:	106,100,000	1929-30	:	115,300,000
1926-27	:	108,700,000	1930-31	:	122,600,000

A debtor country is burdened with the annual payment of interest and dividend. The attempt to increase exports belongs, therefore, to the very nature, so to say, of such a country. A fall in exports is accordingly more calamitous to a debtor country than to a creditor country. But in case a fall in exports actually takes place on account of untoward circumstances in the world-economy over which it has no control nothing is more natural to itself than to try to reduce imports by all means as well as increase exports in every possible manner. As soon as a borrowing country is compelled by world-crisis and depression to offer more for export and to demand less for import the terms of barter go against it, and the prices of its exports, no matter whether industrial or agricultural, tend to fall. Other circumstances remaining the same, the price-index of a debtor country is bound to be much lower than that of a creditor country in a *milieu* of depression.[23] While comparing India's trade balance or price level with that of the U.K., for instance, the natural differences in the kind or rate of fall should have to be taken as a first postulate. Indian trade balances cannot but be fundamentally different from the British as a matter of course. Indian price-indices likewise cannot but be lower than the British.

22 *Balances of Payments 1930* (Geneva 1932), p. 14.

23 *World Economic Survey 1932-33* (Geneva 1933) pp. 57-59, 61, 287-288,

4. *Economic Planning*

Economic structure is the statical aspect in the consideration of a region's economic behaviour. In the second place, there is a dynamic aspect too, and that is furnished by the nature, amount and variety of economic "planning" enjoyed by the region. Economic planning consists in the sum-total of all those deliberate efforts of state intervention in the enterprises of a region which are undertaken with a view to arrive at a definitely desired goal in the shortest possible time. The reactions of a region to world-economic forces like booms or depressions are substantially conditioned by the presence or absence of goalful financial, economic and technocratic activities of the state in the domain of its nationals' business.

Economic structure remaining the same, the material betterment of a region or its economic reconstruction will depend upon economic planning. The items in a scheme of economic planning are numerous and extensive. Mainly financial and technocratic as they are bound to be, they comprise almost everything from export credit guarantee, shipping subsidy, import duties, preferential tariff, currency manipulation and what not to industrial research, banking enquiry and economic investigation.

IV. RISING PRICES

1. *The Values of Cotton, Oil Seeds and Jute Exported*

We shall now examine the behaviour of the three commodities discussed above, namely, cotton, oil seeds and jute, from the standpoint of their values as exports. The survey will furnish us not only with an idea as to the assets side of the Indian trade balance but at the same time constitute an introduction to the analysis of prices that is to follow. The beginnings of recovery will also not fail to make themselves apparent.

The values of exports of raw cotton, oil seeds and raw jute during the five periods (from April 1931 to September 1933) are indicated below in million Rupees (000,000 Rs.):[24]

Half-year	Raw cotton	Oil Seeds	Raw Jute
1931 April-Sept.	142,8	68,4	37,9
1931-32 Oct.-March	91,7	77,5	73,8
1932 April-Sept.	67,5	46,0	34,2
1932-33. Oct.-March	136,2	66,2	63,1
1933 April-Sept.	130,7	73,1	47,1

24 *Based on Accounts relating to the Seaborne Trade and Navigation of British India* for March 1933 (Delhi 1933), and Sept. 1933, pp. 213, 219, 227.

From the schedule the average prices of the exported commodities like raw cotton, oil seeds, and raw jute during the five half-years from April 1931 to September 1933 can be deduced as follows (in Rupees per ton):

Half-Year	Raw Cotton	Oil Seeds	Raw Jute
1931 April-Sept.	555	139	162
1931-32 Oct.-March	552	156	209
1932 April-Sept.	540	157	180
1932-33 Oct.-March	560	152	169
1933 April-Sept.	573	127	154

In regard to raw cotton the value-curve is throughout of the same shape as the quantum-curve, although not exactly parallel to it. The values realized from exports during the season April-September 1933 (Rs. 130,700,000) are much higher than those of the corresponding season in 1932 (Rs. 67,500,000). The busy season of 1932-33 (Rs. 136,200,000) likewise yielded more than that of the preceding year (Rs. 91,700,000). So far as raw cotton is concerned, recovery is visible, then, both in quantum and value.

The average for April-September 1933 (Rs. 573) represents a good height. The ascent from the depression of the corresponding season in the previous year (Rs. 540) has been steady. The price per ton has increased along with the expansion of exports. The price-curve has been sympathetic to the export-curve.

The price-curve for oil seeds is entirely different from that of raw cotton. It has moved contrariwise to the quantum and value curves. In other words, the price per ton has declined steadily. It was highest (Rs. 157) when the exports as well as values were the lowest, namely, during the slack season of April-September 1932. The recent slack season,—the period of maximum exports,—has coincided with that of minimum average price since April 1931.

We observe that the two commodities, raw cotton and oil seeds, have reacted to one and the same set of economic circumstances in two different ways. In the *milieu* of the currency depreciation due to the suspension of the gold standard, raw cotton failed to rise in price. It actually went down from Rs. 555 to Rs. 552. The downward trend persisted till April-September 1932. But oil seeds rose during the same period from Rs. 139 to 156 and further up to Rs. 157. The raw cotton and oil seeds curves ran in two opposite directions.

On the other hand, it is after September 1932 that the average price began to rise in the case of cotton. The rise from Rs. 540 to Rs. 560 and finally upto Rs. 573 was continuous. As has been indicated above, here we have to call attention to the *milieu* of the first Ottawa year. But it is during the same *milieu* that the price of oil seeds experienced a steady fall from Rs. 157 to Rs. 152 and further down to Rs. 127. The recent price for oil seeds was the lowest during the entire period since April 1931 whereas that for raw cotton was the highest.

It is interesting to observe that the price-behaviour of raw jute was almost identical with that of oil seeds. The rise in price during the first portion of this period was similar in the two cases. Only the ascending curve for jute does not continue up to April-September 1932 as that for oil seeds. In other words, the *milieu* of the suspension of the gold standard affected both quite favourably, thus differentiating them from raw cotton. But the impact of the *milieu* lasted for a shorter period in the case of raw jute than in that of oil seeds. The decline in the price of raw jute was therefore spread over a longer period than in that of oil seeds. The *milieu* of the first Ottawa year failed altogether to affect the prices of oil seeds and raw jute in the same manner as it did that of raw cotton. Like the price of oil seeds that of raw jute during April-September 1933 (Rs. 154 per ton) was the lowest of the period after April 1931. Neither currency depreciation nor the Ottawa year succeeded in arresting the decline in price, in spite of the expansion in quantum. The price-curve moved steadily *contra* export-curve. Altogether, one finds that each one of these commodities has its own law of value which gives the shape to its own life-history as embodied in the graphic chart.

It is to be observed, further, that in all these instances during the entire period of the Ottawa year the currency depreciation due to the suspension of the gold standard continued to be a fact of the economic *milieu*. In other words, the decline of prices in regard to oil seeds and raw jute could not be arrested although the manipulations of tariff were added to those of currency.

2. *Prices of Cotton and Jute*

The wholesale prices of raw cotton at Bombay and of raw jute at Calcutta from August 1932 to August 1933[25] are indicated below:

Month	Raw cotton per candy of 784 lbs. each.	Raw Jute per bale of 400 lbs. each.
August 1932	Rs. 206-0-0	Rs. 32-12-0
September	230-0-0	31- 8-0
October	———	28- 4-0
November	189-0-0	26- 8-0
December	182-0-0	25- 8-0
January 1933	183-0-0	25- 8-0
February	168-0-0	24- 0-0
March	168-0-0	25- 4-0
April	169-0-0	30- 4-0
May	191-0-0	38- 8-0
June	200-0-0	29- 8-0
July	203-0-0	29-12-0
August	182-0-0	28- 4-0

25 *Indian Trade Journal*, Nov. 23, 1933, pp. 642-43, 646-647.

CHART 6

Price-Curves of Raw Cotton and Raw Jute
(August 1932-August 1933)

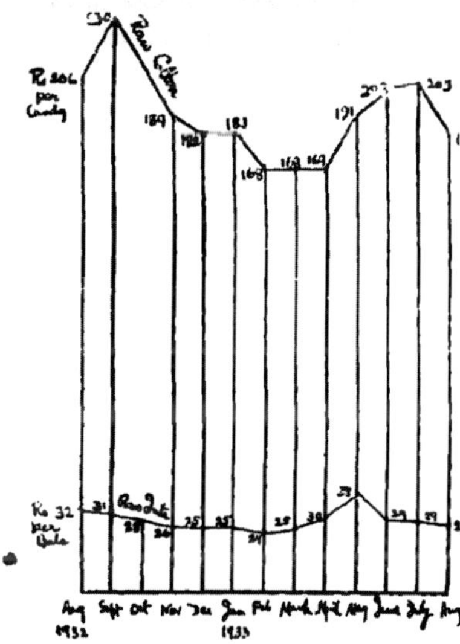

(To face page 59)

(See Chart VI)

The average price of raw cotton during August 1932-August 1933 was Rs. 189-4-0 per candy. The average for 1928-29 was Rs. 373. The index is as follows :—

1928-29	:	100
1932-33	:	50·6

The average price of jute during August 1932-August 1933 was Rs. 28-9-0. The average for 1928-29 was Rs. 68-8-0. The index is as follows :—

1928-29	:	100
1932-33	:	41·1

Jute price remained much more below the pre-depression level than cotton price.

The prices of raw cotton and raw jute behaved in two different ways although the export conditions for both were more or less identical in being favourable. Besides, the same conditions of exchange rate failed to produce the same kind of price-curve in the two articles. Although the exchange remained steady between 17·7/8d. and 18·1/8d. the jute price fell deeper than cotton price.

Under the same "conditions of temperature and pressure" raw jute was behaving in a manner different from raw cotton. Naturally, therefore, one should be inclined to look for this difference in the behaviour in the different circumstances associated with the organization of jute and cotton business. It is neither in the "general" economic conditions nor in the currency considerations which represent the most "general" economic forces but in the "differential" conditions bearing on cultivation, or supply, manufacture, trade organization, marketing and demand, both home and foreign, etc., that the difference in the price behaviour of the two staples has to be found.

3. *Wholesale Prices of Forty-four Indian Commodities (April-November 1933)*

The price-curves of forty-four commodities plotted in the *Indian Trade Journal* of November 23, and December 14, 1933 indicate that the majority exhibit a firmness and a definitely rising trend. Decline is hardly noticeable. A few are marked by steadiness and absence of fluctuations. In order to be precise the wholesale prices for the period April-May 1933 are being classified in the following table under four heads:

(1) Actual decline or declining tendency, (2) Steady, (3) Rise or rising tendency especially during the first, greater part of the period, (4) Rise, almost continuous and more or less emphatic in character.

I. Decline: 1. Wheat (Lyallpur), 2. Tea for internal consumption (Calcutta).

II. Steady: 1. Kerosene Oil, 2. Petrol, 3. Pig Iron, 4. Joists, 5. Grey Dhooties, 6. Galvanized corrugated sheets. All (Calcutta), 7. Cotton Grey Domestics (Bombay).

III. Rise, especially during the first part of the period: 1. Raw Jute (Calcutta), 2. Raw Jute (London), 3. Jute Twills (Calcutta), 4. Jute Hessian Cloth (Calcutta), 5. Cocoanut Oil (Cochin), 6. Portland Cement (Madras), 7. Mild Steel Bars (Calcutta), 8. Salt Aden (Calcutta), 9. Salt Liverpool (Calcutta), 10. Groundnuts (London), 11. Groundnuts (Madras), 12. Rapeseed (Karachi), 13. Skins, Raw Goat (Calcutta).

IV. Emphatic Rise: 1, Skins,—Tanned Sheep (Madras), 2. Skins,—Tanned Sheep (London), 3. Skins, Tanned Goat (London), 4. Hides (Calcutta), 5. Hides,—Bombay heavy (London), 6. Hides, Bombay light (London), 7. Shellac (Calcutta), 8. Shellac (London), 9. Castor Oil (Calcutta), 10. Castor Seed (London), 11. Linseed (Calcutta), 12. Linseed (Bombay), 13. Linseed (London), 14. Tea for export (Calcutta, with heavy fluctuations), 15. Tea (London), 16. Coffee (London), 17. Rice (Rangoon), 18. Rice (London), 19. Sugar (Calcutta), 20. Continental Basic Steel (Bombay), 21. Cotton Raw (Bombay), 22. Cloth (Manchester).

The rise in prices was experienced by thirty-five articles. Of these the thirteen of Group III were not able to maintain the rise up to the end. But even in these cases the rising tendency was pronounced, and the rise, as far as it went, was definite. It is to be observed that of these thirty-five price-curves thirteen were the graphs for the British markets. the remainder represented the price-developments at Karachi, Bombay, Madras, and especially Calcutta. Attention is to be called to the fact that the British curves were almost invariably parallel to the Indian curves. The rising prices in London and Manchester were but reflections of the phenomena in India.

4. *World-Price Indices (January to July 1933)*

With 1913 as 100 the index numbers of wholesale prices from January 1933 to July 1933 were as follows:[26]

Countries			January	July.
Germany	...	...	91	94
Argentine	...	...	113	113 (June)
Australia	...	...	122	129 (May)
Belgium	...	...	75	73

26 *World Economic Survey* 1932-33 (Geneva 1933) p. 323; *Lloyds Bank Limited Monthly Review* December 1933, p. 552; *Report of the Controller of*

CHART 7

Price-Indices as Indicating World-Recovery
at July 1933

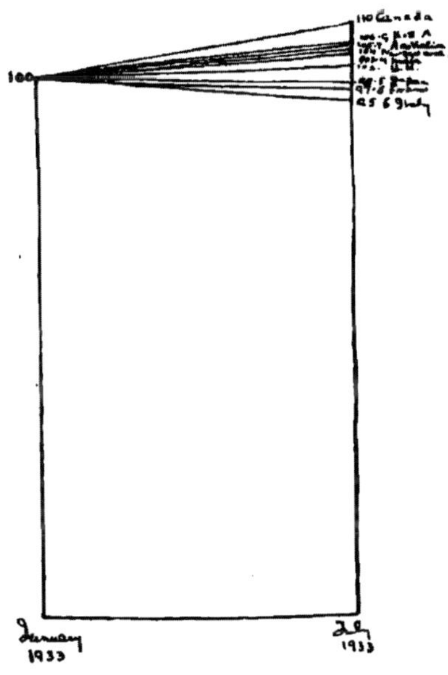

(To face page 61)

Countries			January	July
Canada	...	...	100	110
Denmark	...	...	117	125
U. S. A.	...	...	87	93 (June)
France	...	...	83	81
India	...	...	88	91
Dutch East Indies	...	...	78	75 (May)
Italy	...	...	296	283
Japan	...	...	140	138
New Zealand	...	...	125	130 (June)
Netherlands	...	...	75	73 (June)
U. K.	...	...	100	102
Sweden	...	...	106	106 (June)
Switzerland	...	...	91	92
Czechoslovakia	...	...	96	97

With January 1933 = 100 the relative situations in the different countries in July 1933 can be seen in the following price-indices :—

Canada	...	110·0	Czechoslovakia		101·0
U. S. A.	...	106·9	Sweden	...	100·0
Denmark	...	106·6	Argentine	...	100·0
Australia	...	105·7	Japan	...	98·5
New Zeland	...	104·0	France	...	97·6
India	...	103·4	Belgium	...	97·5
Germany	...	103·3	Netherlands	...	97·3
U. K.	...	102·0	Dutch East Indies	...	96·1
Switzerland	...	101·0	Italy	...	95·6

(See Chart VII)

The rise of the index was noticeable in ten countries. The index was steady in two and went down in six, namely, Japan, France, Belgium, Netherlands, Dutch East Indies and Italy.

In the case of the ten countries in which a rise took place it was not very remarkable as yet. It is to be observed *en passant* that India's index was higher than those of Germany and the U.K. Altogether, in so far as the rise of prices is an index to recovery, the world might be said to be *en route* to it, although no doubt the lingering signs of depression had not yet fully disappeared.

Currency for 1932-33 (Delhi, 1933) p. 46. *Rassegna Economica* (Naples) for October 1933 p. 009; *Federal Reserve Bulletin* (Washington D, C,) for October 1933, p. 642; *World Production and Prices 1925-32* (Geneva 1933) p. 86, also Appendix III, Table I.; *Statistical Abstract for British India* 1920-30 (Calcutta) 1932), p. 722; *Statistical Abstract for the United Kingdom* 1913-31 (London 1933) pp. 212-213., *Review of the Trade of India in 1932-33* (Delhi 1933) pp. 3-8.

V. PRICE-INDICES, CURRENCY AND ECONOMIC STRUCTURE

1. *General Price-Indices* (1929-33 March)

The price-movements of certain countries with 1913-14 = 100 can be seen in the following indices :

	1929	1930	1931	1932	1933
Calcutta	141	116	96	91	83
Bombay	145	126	109	109	96
France	627	551	502	427	390
Germany	137	125	111	97	91
United Kingdom	137	120	104	102	98
Hungary	121	96	95	92	82
Netherlands (1901-10 = 100)	159	131	108	87	79
Switzerland	141	127	110	96	90
Italy	130·5	111·6	92·4	82·5	76·6
U. S. A. (1926 = 100)	95	86	73	65	60
Jugoslavia (1926 = 100)	101	87	73	65	67
Japan	167	137	116	122	134
Austria	130	117	109	112	107

Down to March 1933 there was a fall in every index in relation to 1929.[27] The rates of fall are to be made out from the following indices with 1929 as 100 :—

1.	Austria	...	82·3	8.	Switzerland	...	63·8
2.	Japan	...	80·2	9.	U. S. A.	...	63·1
3.	U. K	...	71·5	10.	France	...	62·2
4.	Hungary	...	67·7	11.	Calcutta	...	58·8
5.	Germany	...	66·4	12.	Italy	...	58·7
6.	Jugoslavia	...	66·3	13.	Netherlands	...	49·6
7.	Bombay	...	66·2				

(See Chart VIII)

The depression in "general" wholesale prices was marked by the minimum fall of 17·7% as registered in Austria and the maximum fall 51·4% as registered in the Netherlands. The position of Bombay with a fall of 33·8% was almost identical with those of Jugoslavia and Germany and lay between those of the U.S.A. and Switzerland on the one side and of Hungary on the other. Calcutta's fall of 42·7 per cent was identical with that of Italy. The Calcutta index lay between those of the Netherlands and France. *Vis à vis* U.K. Bombay was 5·3 points and Calcutta 12·7 points deeper.

27 See the last footnote.

CHART 8

Price-Indices as Registering the Depth of the World Depression at March 1933
(1929 = 100)

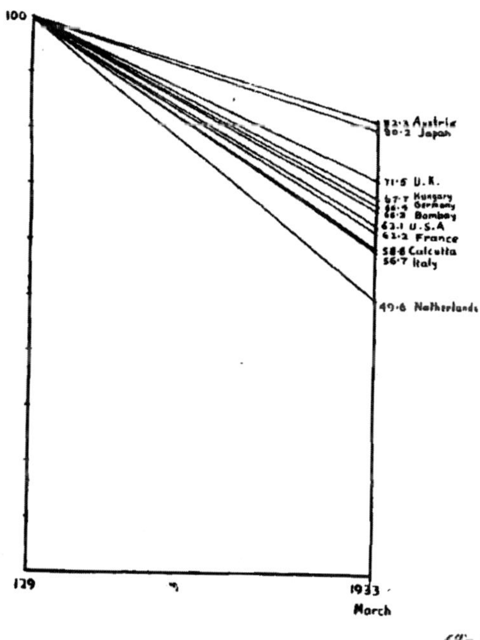

(To face page

CHART 9

Price-Index in the Perspective of Gold-Parity Index
(Sept. 1931 = 100)

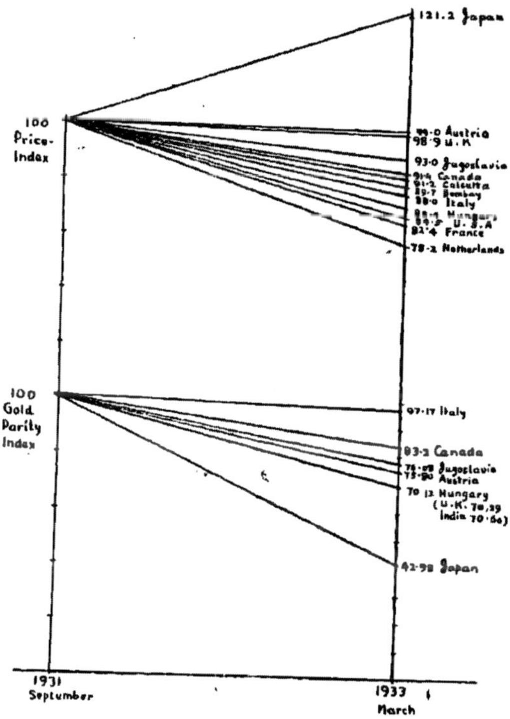

(To face page 63)

With 1931 as 100 the indices at March 1933 are as follows:—

1.	Japan:	115·5	8.	Italy:	82·9
2.	Austria:	98·1	9.	U. S. A.:	82·2
3.	U. K.:	94·2	10.	Germany:	82·0
4.	Jugoslavia:	91·7	11.	Switzerland:	81·8
5.	Bombay:	88·0	12.	France:	79·4
6.	Calcutta:	86·4	13.	Netherlands:	73·1
7.	Hungary:	86·3			

Japan is the only country with index above 100. The other indices were below 100 down to 73·1 in the Netherlands. Calcutta's position was almost identical with that of Hungary and was slightly lower than Bombay's. Both Calcutta and Bombay lay almost midway between Italy which was lower and the U.K. which was higher. The decline in Bombay was 6·2 points, and in Calcutta 7·8 points deeper than in the U.K.

The price-changes between September 1931 and March 1933 are exhibited in the following indices (1913 = 100):

	Sept. 1931	March 1933		Sept. 1931	March 1933
Calcutta	91	83	Switzerland	106	90
Bombay	107	96	U. S. A.	71	60
France	473	390	Italy	319	281
Germany	109	91	Jugoslavia	72	67
United Kingdom	99	98	Japan	113	134
Hungary	96	82	Canada	70	64
Netherlands	101	79			

With September 1931 as 100 the situation at March 1933 is exhibited in the following indices:—

Japan ...	121·2	Italy ...	88.0
Austria ...	99·0	Hungary ...	85·4
U. K. ...	98·9	Switzerland ...	84·9
Sweden ...	98·0	U. S. A ...	84·5
Jugoslavia ...	93·0	Germany ...	83·5
Canada ...	91·4	France ...	82·4
Calcutta ...	91·2	Netherlands ...	78·2
Bombay ...	89·7		

(See Chart IX)

2. *Currency Depreciations (1930-33)*

From the standpoint of currency the situation of these countries at March 1933 may be seen in the following three groups:[28]

I. Countries off gold:

1 Japan	4 Canada
2 U. K.	5 India : a. Calcutta, b. Bombay
3 Sweden	6 Hungary

28 *World Production and Prices 1925-32* (Geneva 1933) p. 86; *Review of World Trade 1932* (Geneva 1933), pp. 12-14.

II. Countries with currency control:

1 Austria
2 Germany

III. Gold-standard countries:

1 Italy
2 Switzerland
3 U. S. A.
4 France
5 Netherlands

The recent history of currency depreciation is tabled below[29] in chronological order:

1930: Australia (December 17), New Zealand, Venezuela, Bolivia.

1931: Mexico, U.K. (21 September), Denmark, Canada (19 October), Egypt, India (21 September), Ireland, British Malaya, Norway, Palestine, Sweden, Austria, Finland, Portugal, Salvador, Japan (13 December).

1932: Columbia, Costa Rica, Nicaragua, Persia, Chile, Greece, Peru, Ecuador, Siam, Jugoslavia, South Africa (28 December).

1933: U.S.A. (20 April), Guatemela, Honduras, Panama, Philippines, Esthonia.

The countries which went off gold standard between August 1931 and August 1932 may be divided into three groups:[30]

1. Gold parity 90 per cent, i.e. Currency depreciation 10 per cent: Canada, Argentine and Spain.

2. Gold parity 65-75 per cent, i.e., Currency depreciation 25-35 per cent: U.K., India, Denmark, Sweden, Australia, Norway, Egypt, New Zealand, and Portugal.

3. Gold-parity 50 per cent, i.e. Currency depreciation 50 per cent: Japan, Chile, Greece.

By March 1933[31] the following countries were still on the gold standard, the depreciation from gold-parity being negligible (less than 3 per cent):

Russia	...	100·00	U. S. A.	...	99·69
France	...	100·00	Rumania	...	99·54
Czechoslovakia	...	99·97	Lithuania	...	99·18
Holland	...	99·95	Latvia	...	98·50
Poland	...	99·90	Mexico	...	98·48
Belgium	...	99·89	Esthonia	...	98·17
Switzerland	...	99·80	Bulgaria	...	97.61
Germany	...	99·80	Italy	...	97·17

29 *World Economic Survey 1932-33* (Geneva 1933) pp. 222.

30 *Review of World Trade 1932* (Geneva 1933) p. 30, *World Economic Survey* 1932-33 (Geneva 1933) pp. 222-223.

31 Deutsche Bank und Disconto Gesellschaft (Berlin): *Währungsübersichten* April 1933.

The countries off-gold could be classified in the following three groups :—

I. Gold-parity 80-90 per cent, i.e. Currency depreciation 10-20 per cent :

1. Columbia : 80·76 per cent of gold parity.
2. Canada : 83·02 „ „

II. Gold-parity 65-80 per cent, i.e. Currency depreciation 20-35 per cent.

	Countries		Gold Parity		Couutries		Gold Parity
1	Jugoslavia	:	76·08%	6	Ireland	:	70·29
2	Austria	:	75·80	7	Egypt	:	70·29
3	India	:	70·60	8	Hungary	:	70·12
4	Portugal	:	70·33	9	Sweden	:	67·54
5	U. K.	:	70·29	10	Norway	:	65·45

III. Gold-parity 40-65 per cent, i.e. Currency depreciation 35-60 per cent.

Countries		Gold Parity	Countries		Gold Parity
Brazil	:	64.04%	Chile	:	49.86
Finland	:	60.50	Uruguay	:	45.84
Argentine	:	59.90	Greece	:	43.78
Peru	:	57.63	Spain	:	43.65
Denmark	:	57.16	Japan	:	42.98

The period in discussion was marked by the following events in the general economic situation of India and the world :—

1. September 1931 : Rupee-Sterling divorce from Gold. Currency depreciation in the Sterling countries.
2. December 1931 : Currency depreciation in Japan. The fall of the Yen.
3. December 1932 : The Ottawa Agreement.
4. April 1933 : The fall of the Dollar.

The "new Rupee" of 1927 underwent a transformation in September 1931 along with the suspension of the gold standard and the enactment of the Rupee-sterling linking. *Vis à vis* Sterling the Rupee continued to be the eighteenpenny unit as in July 1927, i.e. to remain unchanged at the so-called "higher" ratio. But *via-à-vis* the currency of those countries of the world which kept to the gold standard, e.g., France, the U.S.A. (until 20 April 1933), Switzerland etc., the Rupee became "lower". In regard to the Japanese Yen, however, which cut itself off from its gold mooring, shortly after the Rupee-sterling, on December 13, 1931 the Rupee happened to be keyed up to a "higher" ratio in gold because the Yen had fallen more than the Rupee. While the Rupee retained 70·60 per cent of the gold parity in March 1933 the Yen did not have more than 42·98 per cent.

The price indices were higher in countries off-gold than in the others. Currency depreciation should appear to have favourably influenced the internal price-level. India (Calcutta-Bombay) also did not fail to derive benefit, so far as the price-level is concerned, from the depreciation of the Rupee as embodied in the suspension of the gold standard. She was quite high in the list as exhibited above.

Calcutta's position was almost identical with that of Canada. It was 1·5 points higher than Bombay and 7·7 points lower than the U. K. The fall of prices in Canada-Calcutta-Bombay was heavier than in the U. K.

3. *The Problem of the Purchasing Power Parity.*

Now, since money is the general denominator of economic values, there should be an equal intensity of rise or an equal intensity of fall in prices in two different regions *if the currencies of the regions are equal in worth.* This is the doctrine of purchasing power parity in its elementary form, based as it is on the quantitative theory of money. If the money falls in value (i.e. its purchasing power declines) in one region, it implies that the "general prices" of commodities rise there. In that case, all the currencies of the other parts of the world such as are linked to it by definite ratios should also fall, i.e. the prices in those other regions must rise too.

Besides, the rate of the currency's fall ought to be uniform and consequently the rise of "general prices" in all the countries concerned ought to be equal in extent, *if the ratio definitely established is just and proper.* In case the rise of general prices in one such region happens to be less in extent than in one or other region in question, it would imply that the fall of the currency there has not been as deep as in the other places. The suspicion may be awakened under these circumstances as to whether this particular currency had been linked to the other or others at a just and proper ratio.

In the present instance the fall of prices in India was somewhat deeper or the rise of prices somewhat less pronounced than in the U.K.

One might argue, therefore, that currency depreciation was to a small extent deeper in the U.K. than in India (Calcutta-Bombay). In other words, one might suspect that the Indian Rupee was perhaps slightly "over-valued" in relation to Sterling. The justness of the Rupee-sterling ratio might be challenged because of the aparent discrepancy in the rise of prices. In other words, one might feel that perhaps the proper external value or price of the Rupee in terms of the British currency should be something less than eighteen pence. Such depreciation of the Rupee (in relation to the gold standard currencies) as has been brought about by the suspension of the gold standard in September 1931 might be considered to be not enough. Further depreciation might be suggested to be necessary,—this time in relation to Sterling.

But these discrepancies from the standpoint of purchasing power parity are not exceptional in the cases of India *vis à vis* U.K. We may cite Canada and Hungary as well as Italy in the present context. The level of prices in these countries has not followed mathematically the level of their currencies.

Even with a lower rate of currency depreciation (16·88%) Canada's rise of prices in March 1933 was almost identical with that of Calcutta where currency depreciation was deeper (29·40%). Similarly the currency depreciation in Austria and Jugoslavia was less in intensity than in India. And yet the fall of prices in these countries (Austrian Index 99·0, Jugoslavian 93·0) was less than in India (Calcutta 91·2 and Bombay 89·7). In Hungary, again, the currency depreciation was somewhat deeper than in India and the U.K. whereas Italy had not depreciated her currency at all. But still the price-index in Hungary was lower than in India and the U.K. and even than in Italy. In the price-index series Hungary should have been close to Calcutta and Canada or rather to the U.K., and Italy should by all means have been much lower than Hungary. But the exact reverse was the statistical reality.[32] Such data objectively point but to the fact that the rate of exchange does not exercise an exclusive influence on the price-level. The possibility of a differential rise or fall in the price-index in certain regions is not ruled out by the considerations of purchasing power parity between regions.

4. *The Regime of the New Rupee (September 1924-September 1933)*

The "new Rupee" was legally introduced in July 1927 on what is usually known as the higher exchange ratio to Sterling, namely, on the eighteen-penny basis. This had been the *defacto* rate since September 1924.[33] The impact of that higher Rupee, if any, on India's foreign trade and price-level should lend an important aid to the positive as contrasted with the speculative theory of prices. The regime of higher exchange had lasted five years when in September 1929 the crisis overtook the world-economy.

32 For a similar study with special reference to Egypt see Bresciani-Turroni: "Aegypten in der Weltwirtschaftskrisis" in *Weltwirtschaftliches Archiv* (Jena), Oct., 1933, pp. 400-404

33 *Statistical Abstract for British India 1920-30* (Calcutta 1932) pp. 316-17.

During this entire period the average monthly exchange was invariably above 18d. The annual averages were as follows :—

1925 :	18· 7/16 d	1928 :	18· 11/32 d
1926 :	18· 1/4 d	1929 :	18· 11/32 d
1927 :	18· 9/32 d		

The behaviour of exports as well as prices under the "new Rupee" may be examined in connection with raw cotton as well as raw jute. And for this it should be appropriate to study the curves previous to the world-economic depression. We find that in the *milieu* of the eighteen-penny Rupee, i.e. in the conditions of the so-called higher exchange the exports behaved quite favourably. The following table will exhibit the average figures for raw cotton[34] in three periods, (1) pre-war, (2) 1927-28, i.e. the first year of the new Rupee, and (3) 1928-29, the last pre-depression year :—

	Bales Exported (400 lbs. each)	Total value	Price per cwt.
1 Pre-war	2,407,000	Rs. 333,000,000	Rs. 38-11-0
2 1927-28	2,686,000	477,000,000	49-11-11
3 1928-29	3,712,000	662,000,000	49-15-7

(See Chart X)

All the three curves for raw cotton,—quantum, value and price,—rose during that period. The three jute-curves[35] of those days also told the same story of rise, thus :—

	Bales exported (400 lbs. each)	Total value	Price per ton.
1 Pre-war	4,281,000	Rs. 222,000,000	Rs. 290
2 1927-28	4,995,000	306,000,000	342
3 1928-29	5,028,000	323,000,000	360

(See Chart XI)

Both in jute as well as in cotton, higher exchange (18d.) went hand in hand with (1) higher exports in quantum and value as well as with (2) higher price per unit. No matter what be the theory, the facts of trade statistics demonstrate that both export and price-curves moved in India's favour even under conditions of higher exchange.

It is of course patent on deductive grounds that the higher exchange ought to raise the prices of exports. The rise of prices, therefore, as demonstrated by statistics is quite in keeping with the demands of

34 *Review of the Trade of India in 1928-29* (Calcutta 1929) pp, 72, 161, 207, 225.

35 *Ibid.*, pp. 161, 205, 225.

CHART 10

Export and Price of Raw Cotton under Higher Exchange (Re =18 Pence)

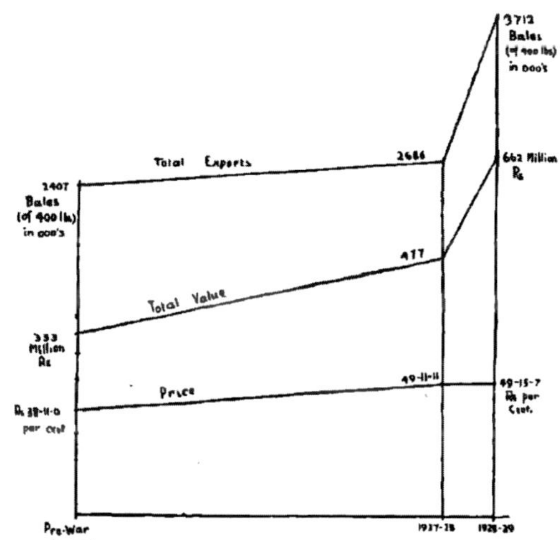

(To face page 68)

CHART 11

Export and Price of Raw Jute under Higher Exchange (Rupee=18 Pence)

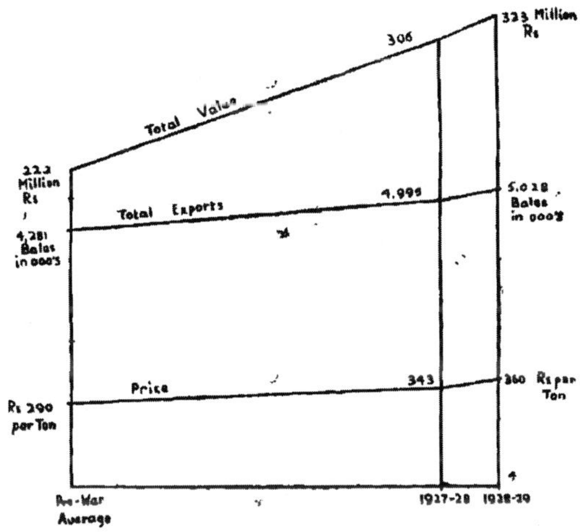

(To face page 68)

speculative economics. But the rise in the quantum of exports is at variance with *apriori* reasoning.

The index number of the prices of 28 exported articles[30] repeats the same story of rise thus:

1873:	100	1927:	209
1911:	136	1928:	212
1913:	154	1929:	216

The reactions of Indian prices as well as exports to currency are then clear. First, from 1927 to 1929 during the period of the statutory eighteenpenny Rupee under pre-depression conditions exports rose as well as prices in comparison to pre-war conditions. Secondly, from April to November 1933 both prices and exports (up to September as indicated in the tables) rose in comparison to the depression conditions of 1929-32. And this rise took place, again, although the Rupee-sterling ratio was maintained at the 1927 level, i.e. under the eighteenpenny Rupee. Statistically speaking, the "new Rupee" or "higher exchange" did not affect the exports and prices in an adverse manner. During both these periods the exports proved themselves objectively to be indifferent to the currency situations. It is not the exchange ratio that influenced the movements of exports. We encounter here a paradox. But this is the most solid foundation of the trade and economic structure of India. The expansion of exports and the upward trend of prices were the realities of Indian economy both in pre-depression conditions as well as in conditions of recovery or gradual restoration to "normal" relations. And these were consummated in the common atmosphere of higher exchange

This analysis cannot, however, be construed by any means into an argument as to the causal connection between the rate of exchange and prices or quantum of exports. The fluctuations in prices as well as quantum were not subject solely to the influences of the rate of exchange which happened to be uniform from September 1924 to September 1933. The only reasonable conclusion that we are entitled to draw is that the rise of both quantum and prices could take place at times in an epoch of the higher ratio, as embodied in the eighteenpenny Rupee. Should this phenomenon of international trade appear even in part to be rather in conflict with the theory of money or foreign exchange it would be reasonable on grounds of factual economics to assert that the quantum and prices of exports are not invariably and exclusively governed by the currency considerations. The problems of exports or relations between imports and exports, in so far as quantum and prices are concerned, may be explained to a considerable extent otherwise than by rates of exchange.

30 *Statistical Abstract for British India, 1920-30* (Calcutta 1932) p. 722.

5. *Agricultural Price-Indices.*

The difference in the rates of fall in price-indices between different countries may be easily accounted for by other than currency considerations. India's goods are as a rule agricultural. The prices of agricultural goods have fallen in every country much deeper than those of industrial goods. The wholesale price-indices of an all-embracing character cannot therefore be relied on in the comparative study of price-movements bearing on countries with preponderantly agricultural goods as well as countries with a large number of non-agricultural goods.

During the period of fall from 1929 to 1931 there was a considerable difference between the cereals and other articles in the U.K. as regards the incidence of fall.

With 1913=100 the differences in the 17 cereals index (agricultural) and the "all articles (150)" index of the U.K. can be seen below down to 1931.[37]

Year	Cereals	All Articles
1929	137·8	136·5
1930	109·1	119·5
1931	89·8	104·2

With 1929 as 100 the indices in 1931 were as follows:

Cereals:	65·1	All Articles:	76·3

The fall in prices of cereals was 11·2 points deeper than in "all articles".

Between 1929 and 1932 the average export prices (in gold) of German mowing machines fell only 5 per cent, American motor cars and Belgian steel girders only 17 per cent, Canadian newspaper print only 30 per cent, and British pig iron only 35 per cent. But during the same period the prices of agricultural goods and raw materials fell generally by more than 50 per cent. Some of these falls are indicated below:[38]

American wheat	52 per cent	Japanese raw silk	68 per cent
Argentinian maize	63 ,,	Argentinian wool	72 ,,
American cotton	63 ,,	British Malayan rubber	84 ,,
Brazilian coffee	64 ,,		

From 1929 to 1933 the differences in the percentage of decline between agricultural and industrial goods are given below for four countries:[39]

		Agricultural	Industrial	Difference
1	U. S. A.	49	31	18
2	Italy	49	33	16
3	Canada	46	27	19
4	Germany	36	29	16

37 *Stat. Abst. for the U.K. 1913-31* (London 1933) p. 212.

38 *Review of World Trade 1932* (Geneva 1933) p, p. 9.

39 *World Production and Prices 1925-32* (Geneva 1933) p. 97. See also

The difference in depression ranged between 16 and 19 per cent even in the case of countries that are not "too agricultural."

The difference between agricultural and manufactured goods in regard to the fall in prices is quite well known in Indian statistics also. With 1873=100 the indices for the exported articles (agricultural) and the imported articles (manufactured) are as follows:[40]

			Exports	Imports
1920 September	...	...	217	167
1930 December	...	...	138	111
1931 December	...	...	123	151
1932 December	...	...	120	135
1933 March	...	...	115	130

With 1929=100 the indices were the following:—

Exports: 53 Imports: 78

The fall in export price-index was 25 points deeper than in import price-index. The difference in depression between agricultural and industrial prices was thus more pronounced in India than in Canada, U.S.A., Italy, Germany, and the U.K. Exclusively agricultural countries or those in which as in India, Poland etc. production and the market are heavily weighted with agricultural goods are found therefore to have their "general" price indices naturally more depressed than industrial countries or those with a greater weightage of industrial goods. A relatively greater fall in the "general" price-index of India than in the "general" price-index of the U.K. is therefore to be taken as the very first postulate of world-economy and comparative industrialism.

From the standpoint of economic structure India, preponderantly agricultural as she is, stands at the opposite pole to the United Kingdom which heads the statistical list of preponderantly industrial countries, as we have seen above (pp. 53-54). Since the British "general" indices are based on a large number of non-agricultural goods the fall in the general wholesale index tends naturally to be low.

The Indian Index-number[41] is derived from the prices of 39 articles of which 28 are agricultural (exports) and 11 manufactured (imports). The Board of Trade Index-Number of British prices is, on the other hand, based on 150 articles of which only 17 represent agricultural products (cereals). Besides, the price-indices of agricultural goods in the U.K. are

Federal Reserve Bulletin (Washington) October 1933, p. 650 and *Deutsche Bank und Disconto Gesellschaft Wirtschaftliche Nachrichten* 21 November 1933, p. 296.

40 *Review of the Trade of India 1932-33* pp. 5-6.

41 *Statistical Abstract for British India 1920-30* (Calcutta 1932), p. 722; *Statistical Abstract for the United Kingdom 1913-31* (London 1933) pp. 212-213.

as a rule, comparatively high, as may be expected. The statistics also leave no doubt that the index numbers of agricultural and "other" prices move closely to each other in the U.K. The following indices with 1913=100 will tell their own tale up to the pre-depression year:

Year :	Cereals	:	All Articles.
1921 :	194·3	:	197·2
1922 :	151·1	:	158·8
1924 :	160·1	:	166·2
1926 :	150·2	:	148·1
1928 :	149·1	:	140·3

It would be but a thorough misunderstanding of price-trends of "agricultural" and "industrial" regions if one were to expect the same rate of rise or fall in the indices of "general" prices. One should rather be prepared for discrepancies as the most natural phenomenon of the price-structures.

The recent discrepancies in fall between the British price-index and the Indian price-index cannot by themselves point to any factual discrepancies in the price levels of the two regions. The real discrepancy, if any, should have to be ascertained by comparing the two indices under a more or less uniform standard of judgment. In order to achieve a comparability between the two series it would be necessary to isolate the agricultural or raw products indices of U.K. from the "general" indices and then examine them in the background of the Indian indices which are mostly agricultural.

The index numbers of prices of agricultural products are available for more than a dozen countries of the world. Not all of them are exclusively or preponderantly agricultural. Some of them find themselves in point of economic structure in more or less the same conditions as India. For India we have two indices, one from Calcutta and the other from Bombay. Both are "general" indices, however. The United States also can present two indices, one furnished by the Bureau of Labour and the other by the Bureau of Agricultural Economics. The base is as a rule 1913-14=100. The other bases are indicated at the proper place. The agricultural price-levels of India, Europe, Oceania and America may then be seen in the indices tabled below (from 1931 to March 1933):[42]

	1931 Average	1932 Average	1233 March
1 Norway	125	120	119
2 Bombay (general)	109	109	96
3 Calcutta (,,)	96	91	83

42 *Monthly Crop Report and Agricultural Statistics* (International Institute of Agriculture, Rome) September 1933, pp. 659-661; *Report of the Controller of the Currency 1932-33* (Delhi 1933) p. 46.

CHART 12

Decline of Agricultural Prices (1931-1933 March)

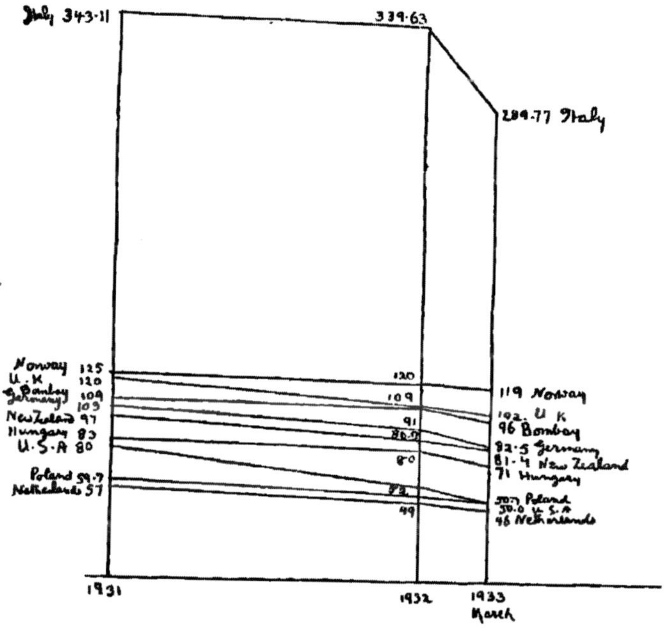

(*To face page 73*)

CHART 13

Decline of Agricultural Price-Indices, March 1933
(1931 = 100)

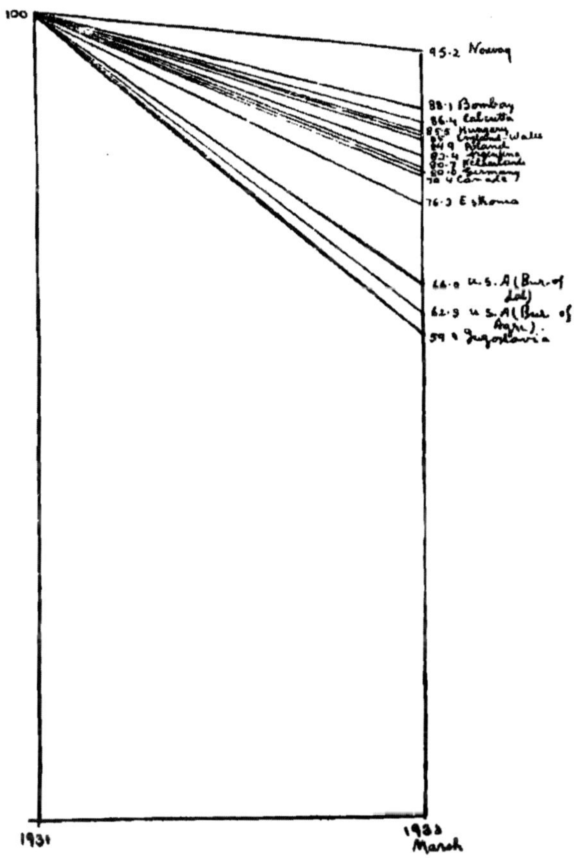

(To face page 73)

		1931 Average	1932 Average	1933 March
4	Hungary	83 (Aug.)	80 (Aug.)	71
5	Eng-Wales	120	109	102
6	Poland (1917=100)	59·7	52	50·7
7	Italy	343·11	339·63	289·77
8	New Zealand	97	86·8	81·4
9	Argentina (1926=100)	63·8	59·1	52·6
10	Netherlands (1924-29=100)	57	49	46
11	Germany	103	91	82·5
12	Canada (1926=100)	56·3	48·3	44·7
13	Esthonia	76	58	58
14	U. S. A. (Bureau of Agricultural Economics 1909-14=100)	80	57	50
15	U. S. A. (Bureau of Labour 1926=100	64·8	48·2	42·8
16	Jugoslavia (1926=100)	97·7	56·6	58·6

(See Chart XII)

We notice that all the sixteen indices point to a fall in agricultural price-level. The comparative depths of this fall can be seen in the following table (with 1931 = 100):

1	Norway:	95·2	
2	Bombay:	88·1	(general average)
3	Calcutta:	86·4	(,,)
4	Hungary:	85·5	
5	Eng.-Wales:	85·0	
6	Poland:	84·9	
7	Italy:	84·5	
8	New Zealand:	83·9	
9	Argentina:	82·4	
10	Netherlands:	80·7	
11	Germany:	80·0	
12	Canada:	79·4	
13	Esthonia:	76·3	
14	U. S. A.:	66·0	(Bureau of Labour)
15	U. S. A.:	62·5	(Bureau of Agricultural Economics)
16	Jugoslavia:	59·9	

(See Chart XIII)

A consideration of profound economic importance has now to be attended to. In order to understand the relative rise or fall of agricultural price-indices in different areas,—agricultural, industrial or "agrar-industrial"—it should be relevant to place the indices of more or less the same kind of regions in the same group. It is only under uniform conditions of economic structure that the behaviour of prices can be scientifically studied.

The price-structure of a preponderantly industrial area is normally different from that of a preponderantly agricultural area. The price indices of even agricultural goods in a preponderantly industrial region are usually adapted to a higher level in keeping with the higher cost of living prevailing there. The rise and fall of agricultural indices in such regions are likely, therefore, to move on a higher plane than the rise and fall of agricultural indices in exclusively or preponderantly agricultural regions. In the event of a "general" fall in price-indices these countries are normally expected to suffer less than India and her peers according to economic morphology.

But it is interesting to observe that the fall in agricultural indices was deeper in all these countries (England-Wales, Germany, Netherlands, U.S.A., Norway, Italy, Argentine, New Zealand, Canada and Hungary) than in India. At Bombay or Calcutta the index instead of being 88·1 or 86·4 might naturally have been as low as in Esthonia (76·3) and in any case lower than in U.S.A. (66·0 or 62·5). Factually, the fall in India was less than in England-Wales, the country which is A, I as "industrial state," and in which the fall is expected to be the least. We are then led to admit that, luckily enough, the fall in prices was not as severe in India as it might otherwise be.

In "agricultural" price-index the U.K. was 1·4 point lower than Calcutta and 3·1 points lower than Bombay. That is, according to the requirements of the purchasing power parity Sterling was slightly over-valued or the Rupee under-valued. This is the exact opposite of the situation derived from a comparison of the "general" indices. On both counts the discrepancy is so slight that neither over-valuation nor under-valuation should indeed be seriously considered. Especially, when one remembers how really feeble the basis for statistical data in every country is and therefore how scientifically non-comparble the international statistics[43] invariably are it should be unreasonable to press for mathematically precise equations in a case of purchasing power parity. It is not the exact "pound of flesh" that is demanded in an analysis of the equations of comparative industrialism.

43 In regard to the fundamental incomparability and consequent limitations to the validity of international statistics see Sarkar: *Applied Economics* Vol. I (Calcutta 1932) pp. 158-162, 199-200, 209. See also Jacobs: "Die Zuverlässigkeit von Preisindexziffern" in *Technik und Wirtschaft* (Berlin, Dec., 1933), pp, 357-360.

VI. DOSES OF ECONOMIC PLANNING

In comparison with that in the U.K. the price-index, both general and agricultural, in India is likely by nature of the case, to be lower on account of the following reasons :—

1. India is an agricultural country,
2. India is a debtor country,
3. Economic planning in India is not comprehensive enough to involve cartellization of prices, protection of domestic producers, restrictions of output etc.

There is a weighty consideration bearing on the relatively lower fall of "general" or agricultural price-indices in certain countries, especially those which import agricultural products for a part of their requirements. They raised their customs duties and adopted other protective measures. From 5 Reichsmarks per kilo in 1929 Germany increased the duty on wheat up to 25 in 1930.[44] France increased it from 35 to 80 francs. The millers were compelled by law to mix a fixed proportion of domestic with foreign wheat. Italy and Czechoslovakia protected their home producers in the same manner. On account of these measures the internal price of wheat moved on a higher level than the world prices. Among other methods of controlling or arresting the fall of prices and somewhat raising them relatively we have the Government practice of granting credit facilities as well as the withholding of stocks from the market.

It is thus possible on non-currency grounds to account for the relative rise or comparative slightness of fall in wheat prices in certain countries while the world-price was falling. The same non-currency grounds account likewise for the facts (1) that while the world price of rye fell 59 per cent between 1929 and 1932, German rye fell only 10 per cent, Czechoslovakian 16 per cent and Swedish 33 per cent, and (2) that German sugar prices actually rose by 20 per cent while Cuban sugar fell on world markets by 58 per cent.

Such methods of control, regulation and restriction have been followed in the United Kingdom also.[45] The raising of internal prices has been consummated by the intervention of the state. The Coal Mines Act of

44 *Les Conditions de l'Agriculture en 1930-30* (International Institute of Agricultnre, Rome 1930), pp. 29, 35, 47, 62, 63; *World Production and Prices 1926-32* (Geneva 1933). pp. 105-108. *World Economic Survey 1932-33* (Geneva 1933) pp. 57-58. André Pavie: La Criso agricolo et mondiale" in *Bulletin de la Société d'Economie Politique de Paris* for January 1933.

45 *Lloyds Bank Ltd. Monthly Review* (London) Nov. 1933, p. 468.

1930 and the Agricultural Marketing Act of 1933 are cases in point. Attempts have been made to bring the supply of the commodities within the limits of the demand.

To this have to be added the Acts and the grants made under those Acts since 1929 in order to combat unemployment.[46] The Development (Loan Guarantees and Grants) Act 1929 is in two parts, and the financial responsibilities of the Government according to this Act are as follows :—

Undertakings	Total Government Grants Estimated	Grants actually made
Part 1. Public Utility Undertakings (Railways. Gas Companies, Water Supply Companies)	£2,348,561	£1.810.98
Part 11. Uemployment Grants Committee	£6,969,000	£4,869,000

According to Part I, 24 per cent of total estimated cost was covered by the actual Government grants. The percentage was 39 in the case of Part II. Grants were made for the carrying on of works in those areas in which the "monthly percentage of unemployment over twelve months amongst men exceeded 10."

Then there is the Colonial Development Act 1929 which provides for the annual sum of £1,000,000 in order to make advances for business projects in or with the Colonies, Protectorates and Mandated Territories.

The Road Fund is likewise to be discussed in this connection. The Trunk Board Programme comprises £9,500,000. Besides, the Five Year Programme for roads was planned out in 1929-30 with an estimate of £27,500,000.

Without going into other schemes we have here altogether economic planning under state auspices worth some £45-50 millions.

It is along the same Continental and British lines that the Roosevelt regime has been working in the U.S.A. in order to combat depression and raise prices. Wheat is being bought up by the Government in order to prevent further decline. The Government has been likewise advancing loans to cotton farmers on condition that acreage be restricted.

The Reconstruction Finance Corporation was established on February 2, 1932, fourteen months prior to America's suspension of the gold standard

46 *The Labour Year Book 1930* (London) pp. 86-94.

(20 April 1933). The Report of the Corporation down to March 31, 1933 may be summarized as follows:[47]

	Authorized	Advanced	Outstanding on March 31,1933 after partial repayment of loans
I. Loans offered under section 5 of the R. F. C. Act (to Banks, Agricultural Credit Corporations, Livestock Credit Corporations, Railroads etc.).	$ 2,075,916,831	$ 1,785,315,120	$ 1,366,998,515
II. Loans offered under Emergency Relief and Construction Act of 1932.	$ 496,025,338	$ 223,709,778	$ 223,294,054
III. Loans under Emergency Banking Act of March 1933.	$ 14,932,500	$ 12,750,000	$ 12,750,000
Total	2,586,944,669	2,021,777,898	1,603,043,569

A sum exceeding $2,000,000,000 had been loaned out to business enterprises of all sorts in the U.S.A. during fourteen months by a Government financing institution responsible to Congress.

The discrepancies in the price-levels of diverse countries or between the home price-index and the world price-index should appear thus to be phenomena of state intervention in the relations between demand and supply. We encounter here the attempts not at modifying the monetary mechanism, the "common denominator" or "general" regulator of price-levels, but at controlling the fortunes of certain specified commodities. The currency surgeon need not be requisitioned in season and out of season in order to rectify the discrepancies, if any, nominal or real, between the internal and external prices.

Currency manipulations constitute but one of the many measures adopted by different countries since the British suspension of the gold standard in September 1931. By the beginning of 1933 tariff increases had been imposed in twenty-three countries. On individual commodities customs duties had been increased in fifty countries. In several countries twenty tariff changes took place in sixteen months. Thirty-two countries were responsible for import quotas, prohibitions, licensing systems and other quantitative restrictions. In twelve countries import monopolies, chiefly in grains had been enforced. Sixteen countries

47 *Federal Reserve Bulletin*, February 1933. pp. 64-66, June 1933, p. 311. Jenny: "The American Experiment and its Consequences" in *Lloyds Bank Ltd. Monthly Review* for December 1933, pp. 501-504.

adopted milling or mixing regulations. Exports were being promoted by premia in nine countries and forbidden or restricted by duties in seventeen.[48]

Recovery in Australia[49] has to thank severe retrenchment in national and state expenditures, heavy increases of taxation, reductions in wages and salaries as well as restriction of exports. Last but not least has to be mentioned currency depreciation,—suspension of the gold standard, which has been in operation since December 1929.

That currency depreciation and rise of internal prices go together has been verified often in statistical records. The experiences of the present recovery also testify to the same coincidence.

The countries off-gold in October 1933 could be grouped into three classes :[50]

(See Chart XIV)

I. Gold-parity 65-80 per cent, i.e. currency depreciation 20-35 per cent

Countries	Gold Parity	Countries	Gold Parity
Austria :	77·95%	Egypt :	65·09%
Jugoslavia :	76·97	England :	65·09
Hungary :	72·36	Ireland :	65·09
Portugal :	68·20	Esthonia :	65·06
U. S. A :	66·45	India :	65·05
Canada :	65·13		

II. Gold-parity 50-65 per cent, i.e. currency depreciation 35-50 per cent

Countries	Gold Parity	Countries	Gold Parity
Sweden :	61·11 %	Finland :	55·54 %
Argentine :	59·90	Denmark :	52·48
Norway :	59·50		

III. Gold-parity 35-50 per cent, i.e. currency depreciation 50-65 per cent

Countries	Gold Parity	Countries	Gold Parity
Colombia :	48·30	Greece :	44·08
Brazil :	46·18	Spain :	43·39
		Japan :	38·28

48 "*World Economic Survey 1932-33* (Geneva 1933) p. 17. Allix: " Le Regime du Contingentement in *Bulletin de la Société d'Economie Politique de Paris* for February 1933.

49 *Midland Bank Monthly Review* (London), October-November 1933 p. 2.

50 *Währungsübersichten Oktober 1933* (Deutsche Bank Berlin). See *Supra* Section V. 2 (Currency Depreciation).

CHART 14

Index of Currency Depreciation, Oct. 1933
(1931 = 100)

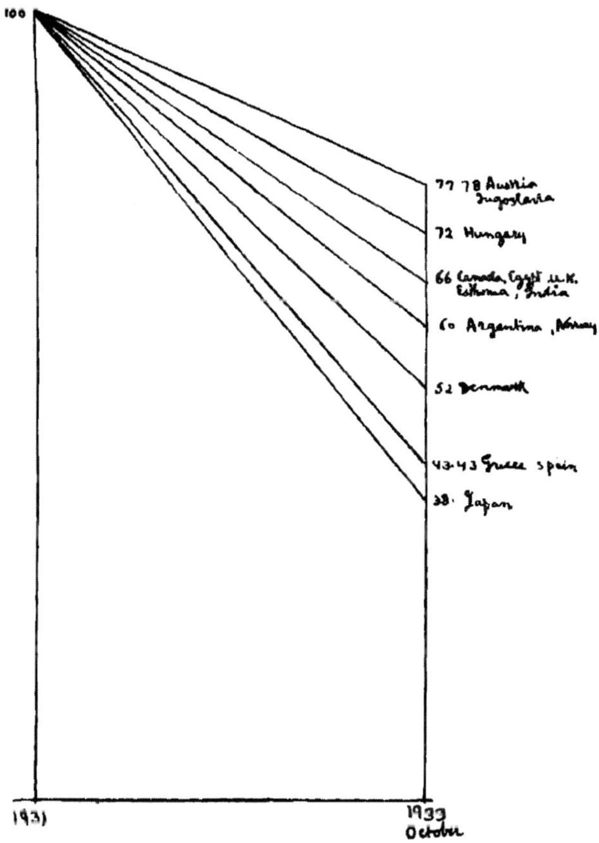

(*To face page 78*)

The rise of prices in off-gold countries since April 1933 can be illustrated from the U.K., the U.S.A., Japan and India as follows:[51]

Month	U. K. (16 Sept. 1931 = 100)	U. S. A. (16 Sept. 1931 = 100)	Japan (Oct. 1900 = 100)	India (July 1914 = 100)
April	99·5	82·9	176·20	84
May	102·1	87·4	176·80	87
June	104·4	92·4	179·60	89
July	106·7	100·0	182·10	...
August	106·1	102·2	180·00	...
September	106·5	103·2	...	...
October	105·5	103·8	...	...

The Indian indices for individual commodities since April 1933 are given below (1914 July = 100):[52]

	April	May	June
Rice	54	60	65
Wheat	78	89	86
Tea	71	74	94
Oil seeds	68	72	77
Raw Jute (December-March roundabout 38)	46	50	45
Raw Cotton	80	84	87
Hides and Skins	52	61	68
Jute Manufactures	76	87	87
Cotton Manufactures	112	115	115
Metals	95	95	101
Sugar	129	128	129

The tendency is manifest in almost every commodity to move upward. These and other instances since the British suspension of the gold standard have off and on invited attention to the possibility of raising prices by currency depreciation.

It is therefore very appropriate to call attention to the opposite fact, namely, that the rise of prices has been going on for some time even in those countries which have remained gold-standard with vengeance since the World Economic Conference of July 1933.

In October 1933 the gold-standard countries were with the exception of the U.S.A. almost the same in number as in March. Most of them had somewhat strengthened their position. Latvia, however, had

51 *Lloyds Bank Ltd. Monthly Review* (London), December 1933, p. 552; *The Japanese Trade Bulletin* (Calcutta) December 1933, p. 3; *Review of the Trade of India 1932-33*, p. 8.

52 *Review of the Trade of India 1932-33*, p. 8.

gone down to a certain extent. The countries are enumerated below along with their deviation from gold-parity :[53]

Countries	Gold-Parity	Countries	Gold-Parity
Switzerland	100·51%	France	100·00%
Netherlands	100·46	Bulgaria	99·78
Belgium	100·37	Russia	99·59
Czechoslovakia	100·37	Rumania	99·54
Germany	100·25	Mexico	99·27
Poland	100·24	Lithuania	99·14
Italy	100·22	Latvia	94·01

It is very interesting to observe that preponderantly agricultural countries like Latvia, Lithuania, Mexico, Rumania, Russia, Bulgaria and Poland continued to keep to gold. The advantages to be derived from currency depreciation were not considered by them to be worth while. That is, not every agricultural and debtor country found it expedient to depreciate the currency in the interest of its exports and trade balance.

The tenacity of the gold bloc to stick to gold demonstrated, in the course of the period from March to October 1933, that internal prices could rise even under the gold standard. The gold-parity of the German Reichsmark rose from 99·80 per cent to 100·25 per cent during these eight months. And yet there was an almost uniform rise of the price-indices in all lines, as the following table will show (1913 = 100) :[54]

Month	Wholesale	Agricultural	Industrial raw products	Industrial finished products	Instruments of production	Consumption goods
April	90·7	81·8	87·0	111·3	114·1	109·2
May	91·9	84·2	87·8	111·6	113·9	109·9
June	92·9	85·1	89·2	112·1	113·9	110·8
July	93·9	86·6	89·9	113·0	114·0	112·2
August	94·2	87·7	89·6	113·4	114·1	112·8
September	94·9	89·9	89·2	113·6	114·1	113·2
October	95·7	92·7	88·9	113·8	114·0	113·7

The wholesale indices of several other gold standard countries from April 1933 on point to the same direction, in a general manner, thus (1913 = 100) :[55]

Month	Italy	France	Netherlands
April	282·2	385·0	71
May	282·2	383·0	72
June	285·0	388·5	73
July	283·3	397·5	73
August	282·4	395·4	73
September	280·7	389·5	...

53 *Währungsübersichten Oktober 1933* (Deutsche Bank, Berlin) p. 5.

54 *Deutsche Bank und Disconto Gesellschaft Wirtschaftliche Mitteilungen* 21 November 1933, p. 196.

55 *Rassegna Economica* (Naples) October 1933, p. 609, *Federal Reserve*

Altogether, the rise of prices can take place no matter whether the country is on gold or off-gold.[56] In other words, it may be quite indifferent to currency and the rate of exchange. The price-structure of a region, like every other economic phenomenon, is reared on a plurality of foundations in which the dynamic economic planning has as much role to play as the statical economic morphology.

It would not be accurate to suggest that there has been no economic planning attempted in India during the period of depression. Undoubtedly, the schemes have not been as spectacular, comprehensive and wide flung as in Germany, Japan, the U.K. and the U.S.A. But it has to be admitted that the currency depreciation embodied in the Rupee-Sterling linking of September 1931 was quite a big dose of economic planning.[57]

The second dose is to be seen in the Imperial Preference[58] based on the Ottawa Agreement of December 1932.

A third dose of substantial importance is embodied in the Tariff Amendment Bill of December 1933, which may indeed be regarded, from the standpoint of economic planning, as an expansion of the previous Ottawa Tariff Act. The Bill proposes to levy some new duties and increase the rates of old ones. Besides, the principle of minimum specific duties as alternative to *ad valorem* duties has been adopted on a liberal scale. A very large number of Indian industries are likely thereby to be safe-guarded, namely, oils, sugar, footwear, chemicals, hosiery, silk, glass, paints, soaps, enamel, porcelain, pencils, umbrellas, cast iron, woollens etc.

The schedule is as follows :—

Oil					
Fish oil	...	...	Rs.	10-0-0	per cwt. (new)
Whale oil	...	...	,,	10-0-0	per cwt. ,,
Sugar	...	...	,,	10-8-0	per cwt. ,,

Bulletin (Washington) October 1933, p. 649; *Lloyds Bank Ltd. Monthly Review* (London) December 1933, p. 552.

56 See *Supra* Section II, 2 (Recovery in World-Economy) where both categories of countries are mentioned as exhibiting a quickening of economic activity.

57 *Supra*, pp. 10-12.

58 See the main provisions of the Indian Tariff (Ottawa Trade Agreement) Amendment Act 1932 in *Review of the Trade of India 1932-33*, pp. 20-23, 246-269. The tariff question is discussed at length in Sarkar: *Imperial Preference vis-à-vis World-Economy* (Calcutta 1934).

Footwear	
Boots and shoes ...	25% *ad valorem* per pair or 0-6-0 per pair which-ever is higher (increase in rate).
Uppers for boots and shoes	25% *ad valorem* per pair or 0-3-0 per pair, which-ever is higher (increase in rate).
Heavy Chemicals	
Alum	25% *ad valorem* or Re. 1-6-0 per cwt. (specific duty new).
Magnesium Sulphate ...	25% *ad valorem* or Re. 1-6-0 per cwt. (specific duty new).
Hydrated Magnesium Sulphate	,, ,, (increase in duty)
Hosiery	
Undervests	25% *ad valorem* or Re. 1-8-0 per dozen (new)
Socks	25% *ad valorem* or 0-10-0 per dozen (new)
Stockings	25% *ad valorem* or 0-10-0 per dozen (new)
Silk	
Silk	50% *ad valorem* (increase in rate)
Silk Fents	50% *ad valorem* (increase in rate)
Glass	
Globes for hurricane lamp	0-4-6 per doz., to replace 25% *ad valorem*
Other globes and chimneys	0-3-0 per doz., to replace 25% *ad valorem*
Paints	
Red lead	25% *ad valorem* or Rs. 4-12-0 per cwt. (specific duty new)
White lead ...	25% *ad valorem* or Rs.5-12-0 per cwt. (specific duty new)

White zinc	...	25% *ad valorem* or Rs. 6-0-0 per cwt. (specific duty new)
Reduced white zinc	...	25% or Rs. 4-4-0 per cwt. (specific duty new)
Soaps		
Household and laundry soaps		Rs. 4-0-0 per cwt. (new)
Other soaps	...	Rs. 6-8-0 per cwt. (new)
Toilet soaps	...	35 *ad valorem* or Rs. 20-0-0 per cwt. (specific duty new)
Enamel		
Enamelled signboards	...	30% *ad valorem* or 0-4-6 per square foot.
Enamel basins and bowls :		30% *ad valorem* or 0-4-0 per dozen (for basins with a diameter of 19 centimeters)
Porcelain		
Porcelain insulators		
Fitted	...	30% *ad valorem* or Re 1-2-0 per doz. (specific duty new
Not fitted	...	30% *ad valorem* or 0-14-0 per doz. (specific duty new)
Domestic Earthenware		
China and procelain	...	30%*ad valorem* or from 0-5-0 to Re. 1-8-0 per doz.
Lead pencils	...	30% or 0-1-0 per doz. (specific duty new)
Umbrellas	...	30% or 0-8-0 each (specific duty new).
Cast iron pipes	...	20% *ad valorem* or Rs. 25 per ton (specific duty new)
Woollen hosiery	...	35% *ad valorem* or Re. 1-2-0 per lb. (specific duty new)
Other woollen goods	...	" "

The further development of *Swadeshi* industries with or without indigenous Indian capital may therefore be expected to a certain extent as an item of economic India in the near future. It is to be observed that neither "protection" in the technical sense nor subsidy of any sort is contemplated in the Tariff Amendment Bill. The influence of "specific" as distinguished from *ad valorem* duties is likely, however, to enable the Indian industries to compete with the foreign on somewhat easier terms, but perhaps at some considerable sacrifice to the consumers.

Since the publication of the Report of the Hilton Young Currency Commission in 1926,[59] it has been a part of the present author's position to argue that the evils, if any, of the currency policy may be counteracted, when required, by the tariff policy. In so far as tariff can save industries from foreign competition the Tariff Amendment Bill of 1933 is well calculated to protect the Indian enterprises somewhat and at any rate afford them a chance of struggle for self-assertion.

The effects of this third dose are perhaps already to be perceived in the revivification of some of the moribund Indian industries. There is no doubt that the first two doses of economic planning have contributed each its quota to the recovery that is visible in traces to-day.

A fourth big dose is now in request,—and this in the form of inviting Anglo-American and other external capital[60] to the task of developing the Indian economy as in the pre-depression years.

59 The relations between currency and tariff are discussed *Supra*, pp. 3. 13-15, 27.

60 Sarkar: *Economic Development* (Madras 1926), pp. 394-399, *Applied Economics* Vol. I, (Calcutta 1932) pp. 291. 299, 301.

INDEX